SHIPS OF
MERCY

● ● ●

Bringing Hope and Healing
to the World's Forgotten Poor

DON STEPHENS

with Lynda Rutledge Stephenson & Nancy Predaina

Published in Lindale, Texas, by Mercy Ships.

ISBN: 978-0-9860284-0-3 (hard cover)
ISBN: 978-0-9860284-3-4 (soft cover)
Library of Congress Control Number: 2012953204

Printed in the United States of America

To each who has been a part of our journey,
who has served so willingly, offering so much
to those who have so little.

Thank you

CONTENTS

SHIP OF HOPE

by Lord Ian McColl, MD,
excerpted from Reader's Digest U.K., *April 2002*

Dateline: Banjul, The Gambia
13°28' N, 16°40' W

"I need a Jolls retractor," I said, expecting it to be slapped into my hand.
"We don't have one!" said the nurse.
"Well, what have you got?"
"I can give you a pair of hands."

So began our first stint with the international charity Mercy Ships . . .
For the next two weeks, we stopped operating only to eat and (briefly) to sleep. I'm professor of surgery at Guy's Hospital in London, but I hadn't operated so intensively and for so long since I was a young houseman [intern], and I loved it. To slow down was unthinkable . . . Daily, people streamed up the gangway for plastic surgery and eye treatments—infants born with cleft palate, faces bulging with tumours, children grossly disfigured . . . people of all ages blinded by cataracts. For many, the Mercy Ship was their only hope . . .
According to a hawker outside the Gambian wharf gates, local people came every night to gaze at the white ship bathed in her halo of light: "They say they can see angels on her decks."

Usually it's easy to feel overwhelmed by the needs of the Third World—with roughly one in four of the world's population having no access to formal medical care. But what we saw onboard the Anastasis *transformed our notions of what ordinary people can do. From captains, surgeons and accountants to lab technicians, cooks and engine-room greasers, every person is not only a volunteer working round the clock, but is paying to do it . . .*

With everyone doing their bit, and a bit more, heroic operations that would cost thousands of pounds in Europe can be done for next to nothing. Well over 5,000 people had lined up in the sweltering sun in a football stadium for screening day. During the ship's stay, nearly 800 patients had come down her gangway dancing on sunshine. This was a ship that carried that rare, most valuable commodity: a cargo of mercy . . .

SHIP'S LOG: 2005

● ● ●

Newcastle, England
55°02' N, 01°42' W

A Tale to Tell

A ship with "a cargo of mercy—"
Patients coming down her gangway "dancing on sunshine—"

Those great images expressed by Lord McColl, one of the U.K.'s foremost surgeons, come to mind as I stand aloft on "monkey island," fifty feet above the deck of the twenty-first century's newest Mercy Ship, the *Africa Mercy*. Below me is the world's largest nongovernmental hospital ship sailing the modern world's seas—an intensive care unit, six operating theaters, a seventy-eight-bed recovery ward, a women's ward, a limb-fitting center, and living space for more than 484 volunteers and crew.

This newest cargo of mercy is almost on its way, and we can hardly wait to have more "sunshine-dancing" down our gangways.

The nautical signal flags are up.

The captain is on the state-of-the-art command bridge.

All is ready for the latest Mercy Ship to set sail.

The view from up here is breathtaking. The sea air fills my senses, and the snap of the flags above me is exhilarating. But it's not the sea air that is giving me chills. This moment has been more than twenty-five years in the making. And I am in awe of how I came to be standing right here—how millions have been touched through our ships' efforts, how thousands have danced down gangways into new lives, and thousands more of us have been privileged to make it so.

Imagine a fleet of hospital ships, staffed with professionals at the highest level of expertise from every nation—including doctors, dentists, nurses, teachers, cooks, seamen, and engineers—volunteering to sail to the planet's neediest ports to serve the forgotten poor, offering all their expertise without regard to race, color, sex, or creed. That was what I'd imagined so long ago.

Most such ideas fade away with time. This one didn't. And I found myself day after day, year after year, in the middle of an idea that would not let me go. Until one day my imagined crew came to life before my eyes and, amazingly, made the dream set sail.

Some came for a career, some for two-year hitches, and many for shorter volunteer stretches of service to change the world by putting love into action in small ways or big ways. And they continue to come, filling ship waiting lists, shaping the future as they wait.

Twenty-five years ago, all we had was a dream. But it was a powerful dream. And it is a dream that continues, every day, to come true.

We have sailed to the edges of the poorest continents, bringing hope and healing, working in the same spirit that guided Mother Teresa and founded the Salvation Army and the Red Cross.

And in these places, the hospital ships have become part legend. That, I could never have imagined. But three generations now talk about the day the Mercy Ship came into port to perform a transforming surgery on the child now a parent or the adult now a grandparent. The stories were told and told and told. And as the word spread over the years, medical screening days in the selected developing world ports became so large that governments began to open stadiums to hold the crowds. *(see photo 1)* And as the legend grows, we grow to live up to it.

The numbers alone can take my breath away—more than 2 million services valued at more than 250 million dollars, with more than 5.5 million people in 95 ports in 53 developing nations. On land, more than 300,000 people have been treated in village medical and dental clinics, and over 5,500 local workers trained to instruct thousands of others in primary health care.

I could also quote you numbers about the need, numbers such as one billion people living in absolute poverty, their total energies every single day consumed with just staying alive. But such numbers are staggering to the point of our being unable to hear them, much less comprehend them. And the numbers don't say what we need and want to hear: What can we do? How can we help? What is possible to do in an increasingly impossible world?

It was easy to be overwhelmed twenty-five years ago; it still is today, because even after helping so many, there are so many more. And we realize that even with this new, mighty twenty-first century ship, we'll never reach every person in need.

So why bother at all? Why do we continue to set sail?

Standing here, feeling not only the hum of the mechanical energy that runs the ship but also feeling the wonderful human energy as well, I can think of several good answers. But maybe the best answer comes from one of Lord McColl's tiniest patients, a little girl who told her new Mercy Ship friends how she liked to rescue starfish stranded on the beach and put them back in the ocean. When someone pointed out the futility of such action in the grand scheme of things, she said, "It makes a difference to the starfish."

Every man, woman, and child who finds himself or herself, by accident of birth and culture and geography, out of reach of even the very basics of modern medicine, is like the starfish. We know this deep in our own souls: every life is worthy. The best inside us wants to offer the best to others. Behind every statistic, there's a person in need of hope and healing. Every one's a story. Some heart-wrenching, some heart-stirring—none, though, you can ever forget.

Their stories and our story—the twenty-five-year saga of how an improbable idea launched Mercy Ships and continues to keep her afloat— are the same story. And it is the one I want to share.

The saga of Mercy Ships is the sometimes astonishing, sometimes crazy, sometimes outright providential history of the last quarter of a century. It's filled with intrigue and mistakes, world leaders and earthly saints, the drama of life and death, the stories of horrors of war and the resilience of the human spirit; and the miracles of modern medicine, human kindness, and ingenuity.

In other words, it's a tale to tell.

Full steam ahead . . .

THE STORY OF EDOH

Dateline: Lomé, Togo
6°10' N, 1°21' E

She's tall and slender, sixteen going on seventeen, a French-speaking African young woman with the blood of three nations in her veins, or so it was eight years ago, when a younger Edoh underwent several surgical procedures and blood transfusions from crew members onboard a Mercy Ship. (see photos 2 and 3)

She was nine at the time, a tiny child with spindly arms and legs and a massive tumor on the side of her face. The renegade mass had shifted her left eye two inches off center and stretched her mouth to an unimaginable eight-inch diameter. Teeth stuck out at odd angles, and worse, a new backward growth of the tumor threatened a slow and horrible death by suffocation.

In shock and horror, her parents, having exhausted every possible avenue of hope, finally gave up. They, along with their village, prepared for her death. And then her parents heard that a Mercy Ship was coming.

Edoh remembers only the blood she would cough up, the difficulty breathing, the fear in her parents' eyes. She remembers, too, the day they traveled a long way to stand in line, how she suddenly began fighting for breath, how she was snatched up from the press of a huge crowd and tossed screaming over a steel gate. She remembers landing in the arms of a giant white man and screaming more until she finally saw her parents again, inside the big ship on the other side of the fence.

Years have now passed, and the Mercy Ship has docked once again in Togo. Edoh has returned for a follow-up small reconstructive surgery, and everything comes flooding back to her, especially the care and the kindness of the nurses and the surgeons. She understood nothing of their speech, then or now. But there is no forgetting the language of their touch.

And when she does find someone to translate her words, she tells them all she wants to become a nurse.

SHIP'S LOG:
1964–1977

● ● ●

Olathe, Colorado
38°36' N, 107°58' W

Nassau, Bahamas
25°5' N, 77°21' W

Lausanne, Switzerland
46°32' N, 6°39' E

CHAPTER 1

THE BIRTH OF
A DREAM

*The most pathetic person in the world is someone who has sight but
has no vision.*

—Helen Keller

I could say it all started with a hurricane, or reading a book about the
famous SS *Hope*. I could say it started with meeting Mother Teresa,
or with the birth of our special-needs son, John Paul. Or I could say it
began with my parents' simple way with grace and mercy and dignity with
their small-town helping hand. I could say all those things about the very
beginning of the idea that became Mercy Ships, and they'd all be true.

Certain ideas and opportunities fall into place in providential ways
in almost every life. As I look back at my own, I can see the patterns of
things happening when they did, and why, and I find myself shaking my
head at the wonder, the sheer improbability, of it all.

I had been imagining the idea of a hospital ship since I was nineteen,
and considering I grew up in landlocked Colorado, that was rather odd, to
say the least. Growing up in the fifties and sixties, I was part of a generation

who wanted to change the world and believed it was possible. President Kennedy's Peace Corps was a popular and inspiring organization. By the time I left home, I was already primed to think in terms of spending a life in some sort of humanitarian effort, just through watching my no-nonsense parents. My mother and father were the perfect blend for the western Colorado farming and ranching town of Olathe where I grew up.

With my mother, it was care and compassion; with my father, practicality and integrity. My mother believed the best of everyone, and my father could spot a phony a hundred yards away. My mother had a remarkable heart for helping needy families in our town and a talent for treating them with dignity and respect that I quickly noticed as a child. "You never know when I might be in that situation and you can help me," was one of the phrases she used to put everyone at ease.

My father, on the other hand, a farmer, rancher, and a grocery-store owner, was a pure, plainspoken Western man. What you saw was what you got. You never had to worry about what my dad thought, because he would tell you. And he told us a lot. "Words come too easily for some people," he'd say. "I am far more interested in what you do, the deeds of your life, than any words you will ever say."

That came home to me in a big way at his funeral. After the service, one of my parents' longtime friends asked if I knew why so many Mexican-Americans were there. Many of those attending the memorial service were Hispanic, some people I'd never met.

"They were migrant workers," she said. "They tried to stay through the entire year, after harvest, and their families were in challenging circumstances. Your father extended them credit when no other store owner would." What was not being said was the obvious fact that they were people of integrity who paid him back, and, something better, they had passed on the story of his actions through their family life, honoring his good deed by making it part of their family lore. When you offer something life-affirming to someone who has nothing, the purest way that person can honor the deed is to pass the story from one generation to the next. That fact echoed through my heart and soul years later when I heard how Mercy Ship stories became family legends too.

So in 1964, at nineteen, I was raring to change the world, like so many others in my generation. I tagged along on a trip to the Caribbean, organized by a group that has been described as a faith-based Peace

Corps—an organization called Youth With A Mission (YWAM)—that corralled a lot of us teenagers to be part of a program called SOS, a Summer of Service. What we didn't know was that we were walking right into a hurricane.

Back then there was no way to know when a hurricane was brewing—no warning and no way to call anyone. All phones lines were down. Before I knew it, I was huddled with others in an aircraft hangar, riding out the worst of Hurricane Cleo as it roared around us. In the streets of Nassau, palm trees were being blown down, roofs blown off, and streets flooded. We were gathered in different venues for safety.

I was with a group in an old British World War II aircraft hangar that had withstood several storms. I remember cracking open those big hangar doors and staring at the sight. As you might imagine, we were all praying and praying hard. We were worried about ourselves and about our worried parents, and as the wind rattled and shook that hangar until it almost blew away itself, we couldn't help but think about the Bahamians losing their houses and livelihoods—and, for some, their very lives. During that long day, I remember hearing about something a girl had said that day: *"Wouldn't it be wonderful if there was a ship with doctors and nurses that could come in after such a disaster?"*

The idea stuck; I have no idea why. I remember how logical it had sounded to me. But I was as landlocked as a Colorado mountain boy could get. Young and all but clueless, I just stowed it away with all the other ideas that can fill a nineteen-year-old's head.

Soon afterward, I recall hearing about the SS *Hope,* the world's first peacetime floating hospital. During the 1960s, the logical idea had come to life—and it captivated the world. A doctor named William Walsh was appalled by the poor health conditions he saw during his South Pacific World War II service. Dr. Walsh persuaded President Eisenhower to donate a U.S. Navy hospital ship that he transformed with the help of donations into the SS *HOPE* ("Health Opportunities for People Everywhere").

The ship made voyages throughout the Far East, South America, and parts of Africa. I remember its simple philosophy: "Go only where invited, and help people help themselves." And I also remember the idealistic way it began, by asking for volunteers—drug companies to donate medicines; and doctors, nurses, and technicians willing to share and teach their skills to those developing countries.

But it was not until years later, as I read Walsh's book, *A Ship Called Hope,* that memory and imagination rolled together.

By that time, in the late 1970s, the SS *Hope* had been grounded after eleven successful voyages. Project Hope transformed into a land-based, developmental program and still is working today, doing a marvelous job. At that time, there were no other nongovernmental sailing hospitals. The ocean was wide open for the Mercy Ships dream.

By the time I read Walsh's book, I was married and living in Switzerland with my wife, Deyon, a nurse trained in the new field of coronary medicine. Deyon and I were young; we wanted to travel and be involved in something to make a difference with our lives. We had reconnected with Youth With A Mission, the group that had taken both of us through that hurricane, and had moved to Europe to undergo intensive language training and ultimately to direct the organization's growing European, Middle East, and African office. But I had never forgotten my fascination with floating hospital ships. The idea still seemed incredibly viable. It had worked once; I knew it could still work. By all that is right, a citizen of the twenty-first century should have access to the very basics of twenty-first-century medical care, and I knew this could be the best and quickest way to do it.

A ship manned by experts and self-contained with its own water, power, accommodations, and medical supplies could go anywhere and do amazing things. The problems of the developing world—lack of dependable utilities or reliable ways to deliver supplies—had always been the catch-22 of offering aid to the developing world. A ship surely could do what the best land-based or governmental organization could do, and do it easier, quicker, and cheaper.

For months after reading Walsh's book, I couldn't stop talking about Project Hope's original floating hospital concept. In truth, though, I had been intrigued with ships ever since moving to Europe. Every chance we had to go to the Baltic port area and the Mediterranean, we would go by ferry. Living in the middle of Europe, we were surrounded by centuries of ship-going cultures. Each time we sailed somewhere, I found a way to get onto the bridge and sneak a peek into the engine room. I was fascinated with ship engines and the sheer intelligence and breadth of knowledge required to run them. A modern ship engineer has to have an understanding of petroleum, electricity generation, electronics, diesel propulsion, and sanitation and waste disposal.

I was also fascinated with the command structure. There is something about life and work onboard a ship that is sheer clarity. In the maritime world, the first rule of operation is a clear understanding of processes, systems, and structure. As a ship nears a port, a certified local pilot climbs a rope ladder and boards the ship. The pilot, who knows the local currents, shoals, and conditions, then gives orders to the captain. The pilot calls out the orders to the captain:

"Five degrees starboard!" he quietly commands.

The captain relays the command verbatim to the helmsman.

The helmsman hears the order and repeats it verbatim to make sure that the captain and the pilot know he understood correctly. And when he has brought the helm around five degrees, the helmsman repeats it again just to let the captain and pilot know he has accomplished it: "Five degrees starboard, sir!"

That says clarity to me. Clear, crisp, and softly spoken commands bring immediate clarity and response, bring ships into port, and keep people safe. Ambiguity is dangerous—on ships or in organizations. I saw the effectiveness of clear command communication on the bridge, and it formed my future concept of the kind of "command" structure needed for a hospital-ship effort.

Wherever we went during those years, I was drawn to the docks and to the big ships, always with a sense of wonder about why, considering I was just a Colorado farm boy. Not until years later would I find out, with delight, that my Norwegian forefathers quite likely helped to build a ship called the *Eliezer* in Norway, which sailed for Sierra Leone where Mercy Ships was destined to go. Does a love for ships soak into the genes? Perhaps it does.

All I know is that while I lived in Europe, only hours from my great-grandfather's homeland, I was mesmerized with anything and everything to do with ships. At the same time I was already in a career with an established international group of volunteers who raised their own financial support for their nonprofit work. As I worked with the organization's European, Middle East, and African issues, I kept pondering new answers to old developing-world problems, hearing all the obstacles that existed for each one.

Youth has its advantages. I was naive and persistent (or stubborn, as some might say) enough to keep pondering the big questions about the developing world's problems. I truly believed there had to be streamlined, graceful answers we just weren't seeing. I was convinced that one of them had to do with the hospital-ship concept. I stored it all away, though, and went on with the work at hand.

Then our son J. P. was born.

By this time, we had two children, Heidi and Luke, both healthy and normal. But an unknown, autism-like syndrome left John Paul severely challenged, mentally and physically. What we could not know then was that he would never be able to speak, dress, or feed himself. We loved him from the outset, but because he couldn't respond in the normal ways, we would have to learn to show our love for him through the hard work of caring for him through the years ahead.

As Deyon and I coped with the round of doctor visits and tests for our new, struggling baby, I began to wonder what we would need to provide for him. Support groups, health care, medicine, day care, and education, all exist in the developed world to help the handicapped. Even our streets and buildings reflect the sensitivity for these members of our society. But that wasn't true in the rest of the world.

Even as I coped with my own emotions about my new little boy's reality, I was well aware of the enormous segments of the world's population suffering with handicaps even more severe than J. P.'s. After all, what would it be like to live in a village in Africa, or Indonesia, or Guatemala, and face a similar situation? The question now had a personal dimension. And as our fears were realized for our third child, I came face-to-face with the fundamental question about the value of a life.

And that was the moment I met Mother Teresa.

John Paul was a little over a year old when a doctor friend in India arranged for a colleague and me to see Mother Teresa's world-renowned work with the destitute in Calcutta. I would have a chance to see how her order, the Sisters of Charity, cared for the severely handicapped and the dying in the midst of one of the world's most impoverished cities. Her work should have been little noticed by the world, really. Yet everyone, from the most powerful leaders to everyday citizens, knew about her service to the world's forgotten, inspired by the capacity for divine mercy she embodied. She had become a shining example of a person who, through dignity, honor, and respect, put words into action, "doing" the gospel, as she so famously expressed it. Action and words—integrity—it was the same dynamic my father had expressed.

The city of Calcutta was a shock to the senses that no description can prepare you to handle. Each night, I stepped over families living on the streets, where they were born, lived, and died. I saw one water standpipe where people lined up twenty-four hours a day to pump their families' supply. Yet despite the overwhelming needy masses in Calcutta, I'd heard that Mother Teresa had instilled in her followers a gift for focusing on each individual as if he or she were the only person in the world receiving such attention and concern. And that, I was about to discover, included me.

Somehow she had learned that my young son was handicapped. I hadn't told many. I had barely begun to talk about it; I was still finding my way. But somehow she knew—it was one of the first things discussed. Only moments after we were introduced, Mother Teresa said something that charted the course of the rest of my life. I can hear the echoes of her words even now: "Your son will help you on your journey to becoming the eyes, ears, mouth, and hands for the poor."

I was just thirty-two years old at the time. I could not have heard a more profound message. She had framed some very basic questions of life: Why were you born? What is your purpose in life? Why did God put you on Earth? What is your dream? What has caused pain in your life?

To visit Mother Teresa was a wonderful opportunity. For me, my take-away was the gift of clarity. She helped crystallize my purpose in life, my role in life and what I was to do. The dreams and realities of my life came together in meaningful focus, shining like a beacon—a ship's beacon. Hence, we have Mercy Ships.

All the reasons against the floating hospital ships concept diminished. This was my calling. As I think back to that moment, it's interesting that I did not realize the potential of my dream for others—that a hospital ship could provide a platform for thousands of people from many nations to find *their* destiny and purpose in helping others. The idea of mercy, the idea of a ship, the idea of launching a new way to bring modern medical care to the most needy of the world's citizens—it was increasingly all I could think about, talk about, dream about . . . and, yes, pray about.

And it was what was foremost on my mind when I had dinner with a special couple one decisive Swiss night.

THE STORY OF REGINALD
AND ADAM

Dateline: Freetown, Sierra Leone
8°30' N, 13°15' W

They said the child's teenage mother died from shock when she saw the disfigured face of her illegitimate "demon baby," with a gaping hole distorting its little nose and mouth, what the modern medical world calls a cleft palate. However his mother died, the fact that the baby still lived was no less than a miracle. And that miracle came in the form of a young man—not the father, not even a relative, but a twenty-two-year-old student named Reginald.

Reginald became friends with the unmarried pregnant teenager when she left home to live with the family of the baby's young father. One morning, Reginald heard that she had gone into labor and things had gone horribly wrong. She was dead, and something was wrong with the baby's face.

By Muslim tradition, the dead must be buried by sundown the same day. None of the girl's family was there to claim her body. Her adoptive mother, Dankay, away on business, would not know anything for three more days. And the baby? Forgotten in a corner.

Reginald stood on the outskirts of the drama, watching, as the young father's family buried his friend and ignored the unwanted, disfigured newborn boy. With no mother to nurse him and no upper lip to suck, how could he survive? Reginald, though, knew a cleft lip was a medical problem, not a curse. He also remembered a hospital ship that offered free surgeries to fix such problems, and he had heard it was coming back. So Reginald found and convinced Dankay she could still save her daughter's child, promising that he would support and care for the baby as his own son. Grandmother Dankay dried her tears and opened her heart.

Soon, the three stood expectantly in the Mercy Ships medical screening line. At three weeks old, the baby weighed just over six pounds, too weak to undergo the trauma of surgery. Nurses showed the two how to feed him formula from the lid of a baby bottle. As part of the Baby Feeding Program, Reginald and Dankay brought the newborn faithfully to the hospital ship to check his progress. In the weeks ahead, the newborn grew stronger and rounder—and they named him Adam.

And as he grew, so did his family. Grandma Dankay cried with joy when they put Adam back into her arms after surgery, crisscrossed bandages covering his new lip. Reginald smiled the proud smile of a father and touched Adam's new face gently.

And when the hospital ship left Freetown, all three watched from the dock—grandmother, father, and son—no blood shared between them save the bond of love. But a family just the same.

SHIP'S LOG: 1978

● ● ●

Venice, Italy
45°26' N, 12°20' E

CHAPTER 2

THE PERFECT SHIP

One should . . . be able to see things as hopeless and yet be determined to make them otherwise.

—F. Scott Fitzgerald

Their names were Henri and Françoise André. We had become friends after J. P.'s birth. They, too, had a handicapped son, but he had survived only a few months. So Deyon and I naturally were drawn to them. Each minute spent with J. P. after my visit to Calcutta reminded me of Mother Teresa's profound words. They were always on my mind. One day in 1978, when we were all having dinner together, I heard myself telling Henri and Françoise of my floating hospital idea. Of the one hundred largest cities in the world, more than ninety are port cities, I told them. And according to the research at the time, it was the world's port cities that also had the highest infant mortality, lowest life expectancy, and the lowest income.

"I think we're missing a simple and economical way to help change that," I said. "A hospital ship would do the very opposite of most ships. It would be a ship that is docked more than sailed. In fact, it would be docked most of the year, either in ports, performing as a hospital ship, or for maintenance, recruitment, or fund-raising. The ship wouldn't be about making a profit, so it wouldn't cost as much to operate, and another way it could be amazingly cost-effective is that everyone involved would be a volunteer.

"People would pay to serve onboard a Mercy Ship," I continued.

Henri listened politely as a friend would, and I thought that would be the end of it. But then he said, "Why don't you come on down to the office? I'll introduce you to the man in charge of the technical side of our shipping company."

"Your what?" I asked. I knew that Henri's family owned companies involved with commodities and grain traders, but I didn't know he had anything to do with shipping. After all, we were in landlocked Switzerland.

Henri laughed. "The man's name is George Rouges. You can tell him about this idea." The next thing I knew, the André shipping family had taken my crazy hospital ship dream and me under their wings. With the Swiss Atlantic expert's help, we began a feasibility study for overhauling an oceangoing vessel into a hospital ship.

Meanwhile, I began to put together a tactical deployment plan for such a ship that would sail from Europe and serve Africa. For the next year after that meeting with Henri, I spent each spare minute thinking about this hospital ship. I subscribed to shipping magazines. I kept finding ways to be invited to the bridge to talk about all things shipwise—learning, learning, learning.

Finally, when the feasibility study seemed to show that this idea *was* actually feasible, I knew it was time to see what was available for sale. I contacted a shipping agent in London, and a friend in Cyprus contacted a shipping agent in the Mediterranean. Almost immediately, we received telexes listing all the ships available. About a dozen different ships potentially right for our needs were put on a spreadsheet for us to consider along with their essential facts: size, berth space, available cargo and public area space, engine type, fuel consumption per hour and day, general condition, surveying companies, the countries' flags under which they sailed, and on and on.

I began taking night trains to ports all throughout Europe to inspect ships on the market, sometimes taking my son Luke as my companion. We spent months, off and on, looking at ships, as I continued to work full-time as the YWAM director for Europe, the Middle East, and Africa.

Finally, one ship from the list looked too good to be true—the *Victoria* in Venice, Italy. So this time, Deyon and I, along with a group of trusted friends and colleagues willing to support my idea, took a train to Italy to look at her.

The ship was built in 1953 by the Italian government and owned by one of the state-owned shipping companies. It was on the market because they were modernizing their fleet. She was one of three sister ships built for the legendary Lloyd Triestino luxury liner company. In the parlance of the shipping world, ships are referred to as ladies, and the female pronoun is used to describe a ship. In that context, the *Victoria* was a lovely lady, with classic shipping lines built during an era that ended after World War II because of the advent of jet air travel. She was a beautiful ship. There was midcentury elegance everywhere you looked, from her grand staircase between decks to the murals of hunting scenes encircling the dining rooms, to the Venetian glass lamps and wooden etchings in the meeting rooms.

But what I found out about the ship was even more fascinating, as we've met people over the years who had sailed with her in her early days. The *Victoria* was considered one of the ships on the "ice cream route." Upper-class citizens would take the Orient Express across to Venice, then board this fully air-conditioned ("ice cream") ship and sail to East Africa or to colonies in Asia. In fact, a few decades earlier, the word *posh* was coined to describe a voyage before air-conditioning was available: The British colonialists decided that sailing "port out, starboard home" was the very best, coolest cabin possible. Port out, starboard home: *posh*.

The *Victoria* had sailed from Venice, Italy, through the Suez Canal, down the east coast of Africa, and then across to Pakistan, India, Sri Lanka, through the Straits of Malacca and all the way up to Hong Kong, and occasionally to Japan; then she would turn around and sail back. She was built as a passenger/cargo liner, with five cargo holds, but what made her seem even more compatible for our needs was that she was one of the few ships built during the time when every cabin had private bathroom facilities.

She seemed like our dream ship. Now we'd have to see for ourselves.

When we arrived by train over the causeway that goes out to the island of Venice, we looked out the windows of the train to behold an enormous white ship—nine decks and more than five hundred feet long.

We were speechless. A team of three Italian watchmen was onboard. We climbed a rope ladder up the high side of the Italian liner and went from stem to stern, down to the double-bottom tank tops in the engine room, then up to the bridge on top. We went down again into the lower cargo holds, all five of them, climbed back up to the funnel, this time from inside the engine room, and out to the "monkey island" area on top of the bridge. We went throughout the ship as far as we could possibly go. After inspection, this ship seemed perfect. But we all kept thinking: *The ship is huge.*

"Shouldn't we get something smaller?" Deyon asked dubiously as we explored the cabins designed for more than eight hundred passengers and crew.

Common sense would be to start small, wouldn't it? But I found myself thinking, *No—in fact, it might not be large enough.* The idea I was willing to give my life for, the idea that felt truly God-given, was a hospital ship: actual surgeries onboard, with all the extra space that would entail for operating rooms and recovery wards. What I saw in my mind's eye as I looked around was this ship filled to its huge capacity with professionals from all walks of life, bringing hope and healing to some of the most struggling parts of the world. With a ship this size, we could leave a legacy in the developing nations. *Yes,* I thought, *this ship has room enough for the whole dream.*

That was the first of many trips to see the *Victoria.* Finally, we took the next step. We needed to talk to the Italian government. The Adriatica Company officials arranged for us to fly to Rome to meet with a Mr. Della Pianni, the Minister of Maritime Affairs. We spent quite a while in the office of this Italian government minister. He asked question after question about what we had planned for the ship.

So I told him in detail about the idea of a hospital ship—a ship of mercy—sailing to offer free medical care to the developing areas of the world. His questions were very direct. It seemed he wanted to be convinced that we were not going to use it for commercial purposes. "No," I repeated. "Definitely not commercial purposes; strictly humanitarian, charitable purposes only."

His response was interesting.

"I am an old man," he said. "I am going to meet God myself one of these days. I, too, would like to do something to help the developing nations." He paused a moment, then said, "I'll sell it to you." My heart jumped straight into my throat. Then he added, "What are you willing to pay?"

With that sudden turn of conversation, I didn't know what to say. When I found my voice, I said, "Scrap value?"

There are all kinds of ways to buy a ship. The cheapest way is to pay the price of the metal in it—in shipping terminology, "scrap value." But this ship was not ready to be scrapped. In fact, we were there at just the right time, or it would have been worth far more than we'd ever have been able to pay. At that time in shipping history, a global upheaval was beginning. With the increase of air transport, the previous generation's main use of ocean liners was no longer economical. The future of the passenger shipping industry seemed gloomy.

But soon, a surprising new industry would begin. Two entrepreneurial international shipping families would very soon re-create ocean liners into today's Carnival Cruise Lines and Holland America Lines, and pioneer today's lucrative cruise industry. That meant older luxury liners would soon be at a premium; all they needed was an upgrade to be ready for a new life as a cruise ship. But that had not happened yet, so our timing was almost perfect. Any earlier, such a ship would not have been for sale; any later, it would have become a much-sought-after cruise liner.

Even with timing on our side, though, we were bidding against a Greek family-owned business whose starting offer was $2.4 million for the same ship we were hoping that the Italian government and Mr. Della Pianni would sell us for scrap value.

To my surprise, he picked up the phone and called the head of the Adriatica Company in Venice. "What is the scrap value of the *Victoria*?" he asked. We watched him nod and frown, then hang up. "We will sell you the ship for the equivalent of the scrap value, which is $1 million," he said.

Then he asked how much time we would need to get the money. In his world, ships were bought and sold overnight. Contracts were sometimes written on linen napkins. Enormous amounts of money changed hands at lightning speed. I knew if we couldn't move at somewhere near lightning speed, this still could all go bust. So I told Mr. Della Pianni that we needed nine months, not having any idea how long it might really take. We had enough for a deposit, but we didn't have the rest. That would

take a bank. He thought a moment, then agreed. We signed a contract on
July 7, 1978, and put down the deposit.

Armed with the feasibility study, financial plan, tactical plan, and a
contract with the Italian government, I began visiting banks. I must have
visited a dozen of them throughout Europe. No one gave me more than a
few minutes of their time. The ship was worth twice the loan needed, and
still I couldn't get anyone to partner with my Mercy Ships idea. Actually, I
didn't blame them. What did I know about shipping? Or about hospitals,
for that matter? If I had been a banker, I probably wouldn't loan money
to me, either.

Finally, I went to the Union Bank of Switzerland. To my surprise,
they said yes, they would make us the loan. I wouldn't find out until two
decades later, while sitting by Henri André's wife, Françoise, at a Mercy
Ships event, why the bank had said yes when no one else would. Henri
had put in a good word on our behalf to his bank—the Union Bank of
Switzerland. And he had never said a word about it to me.

So on October 5, 1978, with a million-dollar loan from a Swiss
bank, the first Mercy Ship was ours. And soon it was towed by tugs to the
Bay of Elevsis in Greece to begin its renovation.

What I didn't know was that it would take four years to get the ship
ready to sail; four years laid up in the Mediterranean harbors; four long,
struggling years that would include an oil embargo, an earthquake, and
one strange, wonderful, little natural miracle.

SHIP'S LOG:
1979–1982

● ● ●

Elevsis, Greece
38°02' N, 23°33' E

CHAPTER 3

STRANDED IN GREECE

The way of progress is neither swift nor easy.

—Marie Curie

The ship was ours—a ship without a crew, that is.

Immediately upon signing the contract, I began recruiting and fund-raising to transform the old luxury liner into a Mercy Ship to meet our own high expectations and the shipping industry's highest standards. We needed expert help, experts with big hearts. And we needed them fast. Not only were we going to do the upgrades needed by law, but our ultimate plans included installation of three fully equipped operating rooms, a dental clinic, a laboratory, an X-ray unit, and a fifteen-hundred-ton cargo capacity. We needed deck officers, welders, plumbers, engineers, and electricians, not to mention basic staff.

I began giving presentations about the Mercy Ships idea, talking about my vision to all who would listen, asking for volunteers and donations to get this first hospital ship on its way to bringing hope and healing. In hindsight, I find it almost unbelievable that we recruited any crew at all. But soon 150 people, some with families, had joined us. Our fourth child, Charles, had just been born. Deyon and I moved onboard with our children and the slowly growing team.

Thinking back, I am slightly awed by this first crew. It's one thing to join Mercy Ships now with years of proven service. But those who came in the early days believed in the vision of a charity hospital ship in a way that still humbles me. Soon more volunteers began trickling in. The work would start and stop, start and stop, depending on the number of volunteers onboard. As the days turned into months and the months into years, I began to worry about keeping up their enthusiasm and, quite literally, retaining their presence.

What keeps a volunteer working? A volunteer has to deeply believe in a vision and keep believing in it. The first is much easier than the latter. During those first years as the ship kept, in nautical terms, "swinging around the anchor chain"—moving but not going anywhere—I had to remind the volunteers why they were there: "There will be a day," I kept saying, "when the ship is full of crew and supplies. There will be a day when we are sailing into the needy ports of the world. There will be a day when the hospital beds will be full of those in dire need of our help."

But that day took a very, very long time to arrive. Why did it take us so long? Because of a tactical error—I tried to save money. The ship, before it could sail, needed to be fully surveyed for $1.4 million. In other words, I could have bought the ship fully "in class," fully surveyed, for $400,000 more than the original price. But I thought if the experts could do that for $400,000, surely with volunteer labor we could do it for less.

As they say, "penny rich, pound poor"; add another year or two to your schedule. It was a novice mistake and, truthfully, the primary reason it took us so long. The survey turned out to be far too big a job for volunteer work. To recruit exactly the right professionals, who could not only take time to volunteer but also could do the work as quickly as it needed to be done was, we found, all but impossible.

On top of that, at one stage in the repairs, we were just flat out of money. And when I say we were out of money, we couldn't put fuel in the ship. If you can't put fuel in the ship to run the generators, you don't have power, and you can't do repairs.

But we weren't the only ones having fuel supply problems. The first Arab oil embargo had begun and created economic chaos on a global scale. Even if we had the money, we would still have had trouble buying as much fuel as we needed.

How did we get fuel? When we bought the ship, the fuel tanks were almost full, so we began stealing from ourselves. We drained every tank so thoroughly, not a drop was left in any of them. With any small amounts of money we had, we would take fifty-five-gallon drums down to the nearest petrol station and fill them up. To make the scenario even more ridiculous, the old car we were using to drive around Greece to collect parts was a donated Mercedes post office van.

So picture it: We would load the fifty-five-gallon barrel drums into the back of that German van, drive to the nearest petrol station, and fill the drums at the pump. The Greek station owner just shook his head each time he saw us coming. I don't speak Greek, but I could imagine what he was saying: *These idiots! They don't know what they are doing. You don't fill up a ship with fifty-five-gallon drums!* But we'd fill them up, turn around, take them back to the ship, and hoist the drums up on the deck with our crane, to fuel our generators.

To give a good comparison, that would be like filling a water gun with gasoline and squirting it into your car's gas tank. But in that way, we managed to have a literal hour of power in the morning and an hour at night to work on our renovations. During those years of painfully slow progress and low funds, we kept moving, from anchor to dry dock and back again, according to how much money we had to pay for the work.

At the same time, the economic impact of the Arab oil embargo was putting many shipping companies out of business. Already around us were older passenger liners who no longer met classification, yet were quite suitable for other uses. Every day, from our deck, we watched more ships come into the harbor. And soon, when we were again at anchor, away from the dock, we found ourselves moored stern to bow amid a row of ten ships.

Off to one side were four enormous crude oil tankers clustered together with only Yokohama fenders, big rubber air balloons chained together for a cushioning effect. On the other side of us was a ship-breaking yard. It was known as the "ship graveyard"—the last resting place before a ship is hooked onto a big cable, towed up onto the quay, and taken apart by men with cutting torches. We weren't there, but we could see it all clearly from where we were anchored.

Rumors began to fly that we were in the graveyard, that the Mercy Ships idea was already a bust. We ignored them as best we could. But I confess to being more irritated by the thought that this great ship would ever be scrapped than by some personal failure. This special ship of ours had steel thicker than most ships built today, including the most modern cruise liner built today, the *Queen Mary II*. In other words, she was "built like they don't build ships anymore."

But anchored in sight of the Greek ship graveyard, I also realized something potentially more serious. I knew the longer it took to set sail, the more our future would seem in doubt, and the harder it would be to inspire donations and recruit volunteers for the cause. And I saw ample evidence anchored all around us of how forces beyond one's control could vanquish dreams.

When you are that close to seeing your one truly inspired idea become real, you don't stop. When I wavered, I would run the trap lines in my mind. *Just stay the course. Keep raising funds, talk about the vision, and let the crew work.*

I'll never forget the day we finally had enough funds to fill the ship's tanks. Two small ships brought more than one thousand tons of fuel oil and slowly filled our tanks up. We watched the ship sink lower into the water with every ton of fuel. I was convinced I could feel the difference walking the decks. In fact, one of the tanks was a bit overfilled. We had oil running down one of the hallways on the linoleum. But nobody said a word. We were all smiles, swabbing up the mess.

Finally the repairs and surveys were progressing once more, and everyone seemed hopeful and upbeat again—and that was the moment that the earthquake hit.

The Bay of Elevsis where we were, just southwest of Athens, is known for its calm waters. Picture a Mediterranean setting—that would be it. So we were surprised, to say the very least. The first quake hit after 10 PM. We had turned off the generators, and all was quiet. Suddenly the ship rolled and creaked and groaned. And when I say, *rolled*, I mean a rather significant roll to an uncomfortable angle. At the time, 175 of us were living onboard. I think every one of us went topside to peer over the railing, expecting to see where another ship had hit us during the night. But we saw nothing, so we all went back to our cabins.

Then, at about 5 AM, our second officer decided to go topside on his watch. He was standing on the deck when the second major seismic shock hit. He heard people screaming on the island of Salamina, about a mile off our stern; their buildings were crumbling. He literally watched the quake come toward us—the earth moved; then the water moved; then the ship moved. We knew then it was an earthquake. So we responded immediately. We'd already begun to store donations, such as blankets, clothing, and water for future relief work. And so, when the earthquake hit all around us, we were ready to help. We moved alongside the dock, off-loaded the goods into vans, and began distribution to those in need.

That Greek earthquake, happening all around us, turned out to be our first disaster relief effort, undertaken before we were even up and running. The earthquake also shook us up in ways we could never have guessed at the time. We were soon to have another lesson in how full of surprises life can be. It came in the form of fish.

We lost permission from the Greek authorities to live onboard during the refurbishing, so our new crew and their families were forced to move onshore. And where did we move? Into a hotel complex condemned because of the earthquake. Actually, it was a lovely beach hotel complex with bungalows only a short distance from the ship. Even though some of the bungalows where we stayed had been slightly affected by the quake, they seemed safe. As long as we stayed away from the condemned area, so were we.

The owners were glad to have us while they contemplated their renovation woes. Every day the crew and I went back and forth to the ship by launch, which was often an experience itself. Our Greek port was a protected harbor, but it had its share of three-to four-foot swells that made getting from the launch to the gangway of the ship an athletic event at times. But the bungalows were right on the water, and everybody enjoyed the beach.

One early morning, one of our volunteers was doing just that. Only a few other people, mainly native Greeks, were around. Suddenly, as she was having a quiet time, fish started to jump out of the sea.

Rushing back to the bungalows, the volunteer began telling everyone in sight to grab any available container. As we were financially strapped, this was a bonanza, and she knew it. So she and everyone at the bungalows with a bucket joined the Greeks on the beach who were already gathering up fish.

Then as quickly as it happened, it stopped. By all accounts, that was the only place it happened.

The fish were of the herring family, from five to twelve inches in length. For natives of Scandinavia, this fish was well-known as a delicacy. We had about thirty Scandinavian members of the crew at the time, and they were ecstatic. Our Norwegian chef prepared the fish in a special Norwegian way, and everybody enjoyed ultra-fresh fish, straight from the Mediterranean Sea.

Two to three days later, at about 8 AM, I was meeting on our little bus with the technical and navigation crew before they took the launch to the ship. Suddenly, my wife, Deyon, appeared, exclaiming: "The fish are jumping out of the sea again!"

Well, I don't care how important your meeting is. You can't continue a meeting when something like that is happening. I had fished some prime river areas as a Colorado mountain boy with feet planted on terra firma, but rarely had I caught more than a few fish in an entire day. So I bailed out of that bus. This I had to see!

There they were again—fish were beaching themselves by the thousands. So, for the next several hours, we all collected as many fish as we could. We collected them in plastic bags. We collected them in tubs and buckets. We even collected them in wheelbarrows borrowed from the hotel. We used everything available. When we brought them back to the outside kitchen area around the hotel pool, we put them on a stainless steel table to clean and preserve them, putting them in groups of tens, then fifties, then hundreds. Ultimately we counted 8,301 fish—almost two tons' worth.

The other people on the beach, several Greek families, who had experienced this phenomenon with us, were just as awed as we were. None of them had ever seen anything like it, they told us. So, as they took their own fish bonanza home with them, the word spread quickly. No doubt our Scandinavian crew also talked about it up and down the wharf, especially about how our chef prepared them.

The next thing we knew, a Greek television company arrived, cameras and reporters from a show as famous in Greece as CNN's *Larry King Live* in the English-speaking world.

"We understand that the fish jumped out of the sea for you," one of them said, and they wanted to know how we made this happen.

"We didn't have anything to do with it," we said and then asked them to explain it to us.

But because of the nature of their business, the television reporters made a sensational story of it, no doubt for prime time. The story spread like wildfire, and even though Greek locals were all around us when it happened, somehow we got all the credit because it happened on the beach where we were staying.

Months later, just before we finally were ready to set sail, a local shipping company sponsored a reception for us at the Athens Yacht Club, where all the major Greek ship owners were members. There I met the man, for instance, who had bid against us for the *Victoria*. He told me that he had bought a ship in Latin America and was about to completely outfit it. Then, on the spot, he offered us a million dollars in cash to swap ships with him. That, for me, was confirmation of a choice well made in buying the *Victoria*.

So, here we were with all these well-known ship owners who were on the same level as Aristotle Onassis and who were attending the reception because they were fascinated with our use of an old passenger liner for humanitarian purposes. And what did they all ask us to bring? Our chef's hors d'oevres made with the fish that had jumped out of the sea.

Whatever it was, the fish phenomenon had been amazing. Even the Greeks thought so. Looking back, I know only two things for certain about the experience: the fish were delicious, and the thrill of seeing such an occurrence was one of the strangest and most remarkable moments of my life.

I had no way of knowing, at the time, that I had not heard the last of that remarkable event.

On July 7, 1982, we were ready to sail. We christened our ship the *Anastasis,* the Greek word for "resurrection," a fitting name on many levels after all the years it took to get this far. That day, sailing from the Bay of Elevsis, was unforgettable. The Blue Peter Flag was hoisted, signifying the ship would sail in twenty-four hours. The last finishing touches had been applied, and our new logo was riding high on our ship's funnel. We were on our way. Tugboats pulled alongside and slowly inched us away from our berth. Everyone was on deck. The ship was alive again and headed to the open sea.

We were bound for our first stop, the island of Malta. At Malta's port of Valetta, we did a nice "Mediterranean mooring," parking the ship with the stern in and the anchors down, the captain allowing the stern to swing around—as if we had backed in.

Why did we stop? We were flying a Maltese flag.

And why had we chosen Malta's flag to fly?

Beyond the professional and nautical benefits offered with the registry, we had a special feeling for the flag itself. The Maltese flag displays the Maltese cross, a cross that was developed by the knights of St. John, who were called the Hospitalers. During the Middle Ages, they developed what they called "hospices" throughout the Middle East, where they would care for weary and sick travelers. It seemed the perfect flag for the very first Mercy Ship. As the ship left Malta, one of our crew pulled out his trumpet and played a salute from the stern.

At long last, the Mercy Ship *Anastasis* was sailing into the world.

THE STORY OF MARIAMA AND ANSU

Dateline: Freetown, Sierra Leone
8°30' N, 13°15' W

Mariama heard shots in the distance as she put her baby Ansu on her back.

"Run!" shouted Mariama's husband, Lahem, as he grabbed their four other children and headed into the Sierra Leone streets. Rapid gunfire drowned out the screams of people being hit by flying bullets and exploding grenades from rebel soldiers. The country's civil war had returned to their village. Mariama watched as Lahem herded their other children ahead of him. Suddenly, a surprised look came over his face. He crumpled to the ground, shot dead. The rebels simply advanced over the bodies, moving closer. She had no time for good-byes. Two of her children had already been killed in an earlier attack. Their only hope lay in reaching the nearby jungle.

Only when they stopped long enough to catch their breath did Mariama feel the blood soaking the left side of her dress, coming from little Ansu on her back. His left knee, shattered by fragments of the grenade that killed his father, made his leg hang at an odd angle. Mariama bound it as best she could by ripping her skirt into strips.

For weeks, Mariama and her five children wandered through the jungles, feeding on bush yams and ground nuts, drinking from streams, gathering rice left on the ground of small farms. Eventually they came to a town where they and others were transported by a nongovernmental organization to a camp two hundred miles away.

Ten years later Mariama returned to her hometown of Mobai, where she provided for her family by practicing her midwifery skills. Her son Ansu, now twelve years old, had spent his life crippled because of his shattered knee.

One day, Mariama learned of the hospital ship screening in a nearby village. Could the hospital ship help her poor boy? They went to see. When Ansu's time in the long screening line came, the doctor smiled and handed Ansu an appointment card for surgery onboard the ship in Freetown. Within days, Ansu not only had received surgery on his knee, but the Mercy Ships New Steps program had fitted him with calipers and provided physical therapy to strengthen his legs.

Mother and son spent the next few weeks in the ship's recovery ward. Finally, she said, after her long story of terror and death and despair, she felt a peace she'd long forgotten. And Ansu? He was learning how to walk for the first time in his life.

SHIP'S LOG:
1982–1984

● ● ●

Champerico, Guatemala
14°30' N, 91°92' W

Auckland, New Zealand
36°44' S, 174°50' E

Honolulu, Hawaii
21°18' N, 157°5' W

CHAPTER 4

LAUNCHED!

God, grant me the serenity to accept the things I cannot change,
the courage to change the things I can, and the wisdom to know
the difference.

—Reinhold Niebuhr

That first sail across the wide, open sea—the pleasure of that voyage after all those years at anchor—was most memorable. For twenty-one gloriously beautiful days, the ship sailed across a smooth Atlantic Ocean, porpoises and dolphins playing at the bow, then transiting the Panama Canal to dock in Los Angeles.

During our time in Greece, we had decided to bring the ship to the United States, where we planned to open a resource and support office to raise funds and recruit volunteers from the United States' pool of talent. We hoped to inspire the same fervor that had fueled the SS *Hope*'s volunteers a generation earlier. We already had an office in Switzerland that we hoped would be the first in a long line of resource offices worldwide.

Meanwhile, we would also perform our first official relief effort. The Ixil Indians in Guatemala had been the victims of civil war two years in a row. Their crops had been destroyed one year by the government's troops and the next year by the insurgent troops. We decided to help.

In the port of Los Angeles, thousands of visitors, including the media, toured the Mercy Ship. We announced our relief effort plans, and soon the donations poured in. That first cargo consisted of twenty tons of cornmeal, one hundred thousand dollars' worth of seeds for crops, twenty-three thousand new shirts, enough steel roofing for 750 homes, hand tools and farm equipment, generators, a portable sawmill, medical supplies, and a mobile dental facility. Local longshoremen donated their services, volunteering to load cargo for two solid days, free of all charges. With the total value of seeds and high-quality gifts-in-kind, the value of our cargo for our first official relief voyage was equivalent to a million dollars—the exact purchase amount of the ship itself.

As soon as we were loaded, we headed for the Guatemalan port of Champerico. Because the ship was too big for the dock, we anchored offshore and were carried ashore literally like big, breathing bunches of bananas. The sea village was an old banana loading port. In fact, the crane used to haul us to the dock was actually steam-driven.

The banana barges were brought out to the ship and tied alongside. Our crew had to ease into a cargo net "sling" with thick plywood in the bottom and stand squashed together, while a crane lowered this netted cargo of humans over the side of the ship and into the barge, where every-one wiggled out of the net to be motored ashore. Then everyone had to step back into the nets to be lifted up to the pier by the steam-engine crane. Adding into the equation the rolling four-foot swells, we knew we were in for an adventure before we even set foot on land. As you might imagine, it took us quite a while to unload.

After our experience in Guatemala, we responded to calls for help in the South Pacific, where deadly cyclones that made worldwide news had almost decimated Fiji and Tonga. We planned to sail to New Zealand to pick up a load of donated supplies waiting for us, with hopes that our presence could help generate more.

We didn't have to wait long. Shortly after arriving in New Zealand, I received a call from the country's governor general, Sir David Beatty: "New Zealand would like to respond to this devastation in Fiji and Tonga; I would like to use my office to start Operation Good Samaritan. We will fill up your ship with building lumber from our mills and with corrugated iron for tin roofs. We have also just trained firefighters in several of the affected cities, so we want to donate six fire engines and will help put them on your deck . . ." The governor general went on and on, detailing this huge plan for us.

Finally, I said, "Sir David, you don't know anything about us."

He said, "Oh yes, I do, Don. I was in Washington, D.C., last year and I sat at a dinner table with a couple from Switzerland—Henri and Françoise André. I think you know them."

The Andrés, again. Our guardian angels.

In the next few days, we sailed to fifteen different ports in New Zealand, filling our holds with relief material for the islands.

While in New Zealand, I had another interesting phone call. An American business acquaintance wanted to donate a coastal ferry he'd just bought to help the Mercy Ships cause. The ship was a fraction of the size of the *Anastasis*, but it had a shallow draft, only twelve feet, which would allow her to operate in areas such as the Guatemalan port we'd just left, without worrying about banana barges and cargo nets for transport onto land. And we had no more than said "thank you" and begun brainstorming how to pay for the needed refurbishing, when the Canadian government chartered it back as a temporary replacement for a former fleet-mate and paid us enough money to cover almost all the modifications.

So, in the spring of 1985, an entirely new crew was recruited for the new ship that was destined to begin a Caribbean Mercy Ships effort. The ship was rechristened *Good Samaritan*, but to her crew throughout the next few years, she was affectionately known as the "Little Giant." By November, the newest Mercy Ship departed on her inaugural voyage from Jacksonville, Florida, bound for Haiti, the poorest country in the Western Hemisphere.

Meanwhile, the *Anastasis* was now ready to sail, her holds full with not only our original goods, but also with the governor general's goodwill operation donations, including the six fire engines on our deck. So we set sail on the Pacific Ocean. By its very name, we expected calm, "pacific" waters. Let me tell you—they weren't. We found ourselves in one of the worst storms since the cyclones had hit the very islands we were trying to help. Two-thirds of the crew were either prone on the floor or flat on their backs from seasickness. During this storm, the sea spray shorted the electrical circuit on one of the big fire trucks we had lashed to the deck.

Not only was everyone sick with the roiling ocean, but a fire engine siren was blowing in the background.

During such a storm, what seamen call a "rogue wave" can hit a ship. You can feel it hit; the whole ship shudders with the power of that one wave. Normally, to be hit by a rogue wave is not a good thing, but this time was an exception. Finally, after what seemed like hours of listening to that siren, a rogue wave slammed into the ship, hitting the deck so hard that its saltwater spray short-circuited the siren.

We survived the storm to sail and offload the relief materials without a hitch. Our original plans after New Zealand were to visit Papua New Guinea, then sail on to Asia and Hong Kong, taking medical and relief donations as we could and making contacts for the future. But first, we were scheduled for a stop in Hawaii. We'd been asked to deliver cargo to help a needy Youth With A Mission project. While we were sailing between islands, something happened that turned us the opposite direction, stranding us again, but at the same time charting a course into another future.

The United States Coast Guard boarded the ship for what should have been a routine inspection of a foreign-registered vessel calling at an American port. Although there had been no previous trouble at any of the thirty ports that the *Anastasis* had already visited, including a harbor in the United States, this time would be different. We were fully certified with Lloyd's Register, completely seaworthy and safe, but Lloyd's had classified our ship as a cargo vessel. We weren't really a cargo ship, but we weren't a passenger ship, either. We had onboard 337 people including 20 married couples and more than 50 children, representing twenty-five nationalities. While they weren't cargo, they weren't passengers, either. There simply wasn't a classification for what we were.

We had come into American waters, with proper certification as a cargo vessel, and now the authorities had decided we were a passenger ship. We had heat detectors. What we didn't have was a sprinkler system, and according to International Safety of Life at Sea (SOLAS) standards, a passenger ship must have one. That might sound like a small thing to add. But on a ship the size of the *Anastasis,* that would include retrofitting several miles of steel pipe and sprinkler heads at the cost of a million dollars.

After all the years in Greece, this was quite a blow. We had a choice: we could lift the anchors and sail straight to Hong Kong and never return to U.S. waters, or we could do whatever the U.S. authorities wanted us to do. But really, there was no choice. Once a shadow is cast over how you operate a ship, you'll always have a problem. For the sake of the hospital ship future we still believed in so deeply, we decided to comply.

We pulled into Honolulu, set anchor, and moved all the families ashore to live in three different campgrounds while we began upgrading to meet the SOLAS standards. Eighteen months passed before we headed to sea again toward British Columbia to complete the final modifications required to gain passenger certification.

And in the midst of it all, I received the strangest call of my life.

THE STORY OF DAISY

Excerpted from *Mercy Ships News*,
Asian Edition, Spring 2000

Dateline: Pulupandan, Philippines
10°31' N, 122°48' E

Hiding behind oversized sunglasses, Daisy shyly entered the orthopedic screening exam room. With her mother by her side, the 20-year-old waited quietly while Mercy Ships orthopedic surgeon Dr. Tim Browne examined her arms and legs. Finding no orthopedic problems, Dr. Tim asked her to remove the dark glasses that concealed her eyes. Shocked, he looked into the disfigured face of the young woman. Scars from a botched cleft palate surgery she had received as a child distorted her lower eyelids, turning them down and under. Daisy could not close her eyes.

Dr. Browne felt instant compassion for her, but without an ophthalmologist trained in plastic surgery, a rare combination, there was little the Caribbean Mercy *crew could do to help her.*

So Dr. Browne referred Daisy to the Mercy Ships optical screening clinic, hoping that at least she could receive a new pair of glasses for her failing eyesight. There she was examined and asked to return the following week.

Meanwhile, Dr. Rafael Rodriguez, an ophthalmologist from Manila, had arrived to volunteer with the ship's floating eye surgery hospital for a few days. When the ophthalmologist examined Daisy, everyone was in for a surprise. What no one on the Caribbean Mercy *knew was that Dr. Rodriguez was trained in ophthalmic plastic surgery, precisely the kind of surgery Daisy needed.*

Daisy, though, would need to travel to Manila for the surgery, where Dr. Rodriquez could arrange to do the reconstructive procedure. Other friends of Mercy Ships, Congressman Charlie Cojuangco and his wife, Vice Mayor Rio, volunteered to sponsor Daisy's flight to Manila.

Skin grafts from behind Daisy's ears were used to patch the facial area, restoring her eyes to normal shape. For the first time in her life, Daisy was able to close her tired eyes.

Back home, recovered fully, Daisy discovered a normal life waiting for her, with the wonder of eyes that could close and a face she could show to the world.

SHIP'S LOG:
1984–1986

● ● ●

Athens, Greece
37°58' N, 23°43' E

CHAPTER 5

ON TRIAL
IN GREECE

All the great things are simple, and many can be expressed in a single word: freedom; justice; honor; duty; hope; mercy.

—Sir Winston Churchill

Almost three years after we had sailed from Greece, as the *Anastasis* sat in yet another bay "swinging around our anchor chain," I received a shore-to-ship phone call from Costas Macris, a friend in Athens, informing me that my name appeared on a docket along with his in an Athens court.

To say I was shocked is an enormous understatement, not only for myself, but also for Costas.

Costas Macris was from a well-known family in Greece. His uncle was a sculptor famous enough to have his work prominently placed in the Athens Museum of Modern Sculpture. A Presbyterian pastor, Costas had befriended us while we worked to make the *Anastasis* seaworthy.

The rest of his words sank in very slowly: also on the docket was the name of another crew leader onboard, Alan Williams, a British citizen from New Zealand. The Greek authorities had not even bothered to notify us. Costas told me that I'd be involved in the trial in absentia, so there was nothing to worry about. He told me he was requesting a delay in the trial. As non-Greek citizens, we didn't have to return to stand trial, but as a Greek, he did. The question that hung in the air as we talked was obvious: Would I consider returning to Athens, bringing Alan with me? Otherwise, Costas would stand trial alone.

And if I wasn't shocked before, I was certainly shocked to hear the charges—proselytism and attempted psychological abduction of a minor. Costas explained that the charges were being brought by the mother of a young man named Kostas Kotopoulos. I remembered the teenager. We met both the father and son while doing earthquake relief work. His parents were divorced, and the boy was living with his father. I remembered his father telling some of our group how his son was "mesmerized" by the ship.

"My son really wants to learn English, and he likes playing with your children. Do you mind if I bring him to the ship from time to time?" the father had asked. The boy was about the same age as my daughter and some of the other children. We could see that he was incredibly bright and curious. Sure, we had told the father. His son could visit anytime.

As for my friend Costas Macris, he was well-known in Greece for another interesting accomplishment. His family had taken the *Living Bible*, which was a worldwide phenomenon at the time, and translated parts of it into modern Greek. Controversy accompanied the whole idea of a Bible in modern vernacular, but most Christians around the world embraced it, especially young people. Macris's modern Greek *Living Bible* was a best-seller in the country in the early eighties. So Macris was well-known, his family was well-known, but what I didn't know was, *we* were well-known. We weren't well-known because of the earthquake relief effort; it was because of the fish jumping from the sea.

I was intrigued to learn that a surprising number of Greek citizens still recalled the television coverage of that fish event, but not in an accurate way. The Greek television crew had made the fish story about us, not the remarkable fish phenomenon. We were the ship and crew that had sailed into port and made the fish jump from the sea. I tried to put myself in the mother's shoes. With all that dramatic and memorable press coverage, did she begin to wonder about this "strange" foreign ship and the crew's effect on her son? Perhaps. Considering that the son in question was now nineteen, an adult under Greek law, and currently working in his father's business, why did it matter? The ship and her crew were now half a world away; two years had passed. Greece, to me, was already a fading memory.

I could only assume that was the psychological abduction part of the accusation. The proselytizing charge somehow must have been related to Costas Macris's Greek translation of the *Living Bible* and the box of them he had given us for the earthquake relief work—plus the fact that we were not Greek Orthodox, the state-funded religion of Greece.

Accusations of proselytism were a real problem in Greece. They had become an almost common occurrence. Greece, with its incredibly rich and complex history, had laws still on the books meant to protect the state church and, therefore, protect the Greek way of life and faith. That was especially the case during the early twentieth century, when Greece was reestablishing its national independence after centuries of Muslim rule.

Of course, we didn't know much of this, so we took this charge very badly. Mercy Ships had crew and volunteers from every walk of life. We were learning daily that cultural respect was part of such diversity. Although Mercy Ships values were deeply rooted in the Christian faith, my growing vision, especially after meeting Mother Teresa, was that we were going to be more about love in action, less about words, similar to other charities, such as the Salvation Army.

I realized early on that if we allowed medicine to become the heart of the ship, then every port in the world would open to us. If not, many doors would close, and the poorest of the poor would never be able to receive what we alone might be able to offer them. So I considered the situation carefully, turning it over in my mind. From my viewpoint, no one onboard was trying to change the boy's religion. After all, he was already a Greek Orthodox Christian. The boy we met, whose father asked if he could spend time with us on the ship to practice his English and hang out with our kids, was a teenager with the normal teenage issues, who seemed also rather lonely, as many teenagers of divorced parents are. Our crew clearly recalled giving a copy of Costas's translated *Living Bible* to comfort and encourage the boy in the same spirit we handed out copies during the recent earthquake relief work.

Even though I had lived in a Greek harbor for three years, I was beginning to realize how little I understood the country's culture or its laws. I just knew the charges weren't true. As an American reared to be-lieve that freedom to choose one's own religion was a basic human right, I also fought a feeling of outrage at the whole situation.

But most of all, I worried about my friend who wanted to clear his name so much that he'd go to court over such a strange accusation, my friend who did not expect me to come back.

So why could I not quit wondering if I should?

To go back made no sense on almost every level. I had a family to support, not to mention a fledgling organization that was struggling to fulfill its true potential. "In absentia" all but states the expectations of a "no-show." The fact that neither of us had been notified also spoke vol-umes. I didn't want to be naive about it. I had heard enough stories about the absence of justice in political systems around the world to know that anything was a possibility. But I couldn't stop thinking about Greece and about Costas Macris.

So I found myself discussing this at Thanksgiving a few weeks later with my brother, sister, and parents. Mercy Ships was once again at a critical stage, I pointed out. I was American, not Greek. These were not my laws, so, wasn't this really a matter between Costas and his country's legal system? After all, what would happen to my family if I went to jail because of the lack of religious freedom in another nation? And not just any nation, but a nation considered to be the very cradle of democracy? It made no sense from any angle.

After a few minutes, my dad said, "Son, I don't know why we are even discussing this."

"Why is that, Dad?" I asked.

"Because I have always taught you to do what is right, and what is right is that you go back and stand with that friend of yours who *is* Greek and doesn't have the luxury you do of choosing whether to face this crisis or not."

Dad summarized what was bothering me.

For Costas, a guilty verdict would damage his reputation, at best; at worst, he could actually see prison time for things the rest of us hold so dear—justice and religious freedom. The least I could do for Costas Mac-ris, who had helped Mercy Ships during our slow, slow years in Greece, was to go back and testify in his behalf. As it turned out, Alan had come to the same conclusion.

That's when the surprises began!

To the surprise of everyone, we made plans to return.

To the surprise of the Greek authorities, we showed up and testified at the trial.

To our surprise, we were all found **guilty**.

But the guilty verdict wasn't a surprise to the Greeks. Proselytism accusations were so common that some attorneys actually specialized in them. Our next attorney, a Catholic, had represented more proselytism cases than any other attorney in the country—the problem was he hadn't won a single one, nor had anyone, to my knowledge. The abuse of proselytism laws was one of Greece's major problems of the day, a court system dealing with old laws creating damaging prejudice that was playing out much like our racial prejudice in the United States, but this prejudice was playing out along cultural lines. For instance, we soon learned that neither Protestants nor Catholics could be schoolteachers or officers in the Greek army.

Long-held social lines were being tested here, just as they were around the world. And Costas, Alan, and I had been caught in the middle.

After being found guilty, we were sentenced to three and a half years in prison.

I thought we would go straight to jail. Instead, the appeal process began on the spot. We surrendered our passports for documentation, and to our surprise, the judge returned them immediately. He said Alan and I were free to go, but that we would be added to the docket of the appellate court schedule. Then the judge made it crystal clear that if the appellate court upheld the lower court's finding, we would have only one more appeal, and that would be to the Greek Supreme Court. But—and this was a *big* but— if we were found guilty at the appellate court level, we would go straight to jail.

Think about it. We were handed back our passports and told to go home and come back in eighteen months for another trial that, if we lost, would mean we'd go straight to prison. That told me that the Greek authorities wanted us to stay this time "in absentia."

But of course, we again went back. The decision, this time, wasn't as easy or as quick in coming. Deyon and I went through the process of adding three and a half years to the ages of each of our kids. That was an eye-opener. Was this foolhardy? Again, what about Mercy Ships? We had two ships and about 350 staff by that time. Wasn't that more important? Would this still be "doing the right thing," as my father had first said? A prison sentence is as real as a reality check gets. After all, just because it was right in one instance didn't mean it was automatically right in the next.

And yet Alan and I decided we should go back.

But this time, we were prepared.

When Alan and I left Greece after the first trial, we went straight home and contacted both the British and the U.S. embassies. We mounted a massive public relations campaign and produced a mound of petitions signed and delivered to the Greek embassies in Washington and every Western European nation. More than four hundred thousand Americans alone signed petitions to Greek Prime Minister Papendreou. U.S. congressmen sent letters to the Greek government. California Governor Deukmejian wrote Greek President Sartzetakis and so did President Ronald Reagan.

The argument went something like this: How is this possible? Greece is signatory to the United Nations Declaration of Human Rights, and one of the most basic rights is the freedom to choose one's own faith without penalty. How could that not be an option in the nation that considers itself the birthplace of the democratic system?

Soon we learned that others in Greece began to see this case as one that could help change these outmoded laws to more accurately reflect the modern Greek thinking. We suddenly realized we were becoming involved in something bigger than ourselves, and in a detached, intellectual way, I became fascinated with what I was learning about international justice and human rights. With Mercy Ships always on my mind, especially as I contemplated its future, as well as my own, I couldn't help, even then, seeing how the same sort of injustices might play out in the developing world.

On May 21, my wife's fortieth birthday, the court case began in Athens. Alan and I, along with Deyon and two of our children, flew back to Greece to join Costas Macris before the three-judge panel set to decide the case.

The witnesses for our defense began lining up. A former director of studies at the International Institute of Human Rights in Strasbourg, France, testified as an expert on human rights. The International Commission of Jurists sent an observer to ensure that the human rights of the defendants were upheld.

The daughter of a former prime minister, a professor of law at Athens University, testified on our behalf, and so did two Greek Orthodox priests. One of the priests said, "These nonorthodox were the first ones to respond after our earthquake, bringing blankets and clothing and food and potable water. We have partnered with them; we know these people are not like they are made out to be."

"This is not even an issue with the Orthodox church," the other said. "This has been politicized. Costas Macris was only doing what the church is supposed to do for its youth."

Amazingly enough, even the Greek public prosecutor told the judges that, in his opinion, the state had made a mistake in prosecuting the case, since it was neither factually nor legally true.

The verdict from the three-judge panel came quickly just after midnight on the fifth day of the trial—**not guilty**. We were free to go, and Costas's name had been cleared.

After this case, I was told that the laws began to slowly change, that Greeks of all faiths soon were able to become army officers and teachers. I was also told that if we had lost, the case would have gone to the European Court of Human Rights. The legal arguments opposing the Greek anti-proselytizing law were used in other cases.

On a personal level, it would take me years to process what happened. While justice did ultimately prevail for me, I went home resolved to understand what justice really meant in the context of everyday work and life. In the years to come, as we moved forward with Mercy Ships, I became determined to root all our efforts in a deep sense of justice—physically, economically, emotionally, spiritually, and legally.

There's another chapter to the story, by the way. A few years after the trial, the boy involved—Kostas—contacted us. By that time, he was even more multilingual, eventually becoming fluent in five languages and earning two graduate degrees abroad. He had recently found himself thinking again and again about the Mercy Ship he'd visited so often as a boy. That was why he had called. He asked me for a job, then and there. With his linguistic and developmental skills, not to mention the drama of our lives intertwining, how could I say no?

I CAN SEE!

Excerpted from *Mercy Ships Newsletter*,
North American edition, Summer 1987

Dateline: February 17, 1987
Lazaro Cardenas, Mexico
17°53' N, 102°12' W

Señora Refugio Camacho shuffled up the gangway, her daughter hovering by her side, the rolling and rocking of the ship feeling, no doubt, like the recent earthquake. The ship's crew gathered near the gangway, wanting to catch a glimpse of their first surgery patient.

She was 68 years old, face lined, grey wisps of hair escaping from her bun, hands calloused and arthritic, eyes dull with fading years and cloudy with cataracts. And she was stepping into a strange world, a big hospital ship that had anchored near her home after the Mexico earthquake.

With a red ink thumbprint, she signed the patient consent form, donned a yellow paper gown and surgical cap, and with a final shaky smile at her daughter's retreating touch, she was led into surgery. An assortment of medical professionals from Mexico and around the world who had arrived after Mercy Ships put out a call for expert help, all crowded into the room for this history in the making as Dr. Bob Dyer performed the cataract surgery.

And that was also the scene the next morning as well, as everyone excitedly gathered around Señora Camacho to watch Dr. Dyer carefully remove the eye patch. As the first eye patch fell away, Señora Camacho looked toward her daughter and gasped, "Yo puedo ver! Yo puedo ver!" I can see! I can see! She grabbed Dr. Dyer's hand, "Gracias! Gracias!"

The Mercy Ship was now, finally, a hospital ship.

SHIP'S LOG:
1986–1987

● ● ●

Lazaro Cardenas, Mexico
17°05' N, 102°12' W

CHAPTER 6

A TRUE HOSPITAL SHIP

Whoever is spared personal pain must feel himself called to help in diminishing the pain of others.

—Albert Schweitzer

When I returned from Greece, I came back ready to see Mercy Ships finally become what I'd first envisioned so long ago. Before Hawaii, I had allowed the hospital ship vision, the idea that came into clear-eyed focus after meeting Mother Teresa, to be postponed by calls for relief work, all worthy efforts but not my original vision. Being a relief ship was a marvelous thing, but I knew others could do that. In my heart, the dream I was willing to give my life for was the dream of a fleet of hospital ships.

That was what was on my mind when I heard about the Mexico City earthquake only weeks after my return. The passenger upgrades almost finished, the *Anastasis* was now in British Columbia, finishing the last bits of work to gain the SOLAS certification. It would soon be time to sail again. So I went to Mexico to investigate an invitation by the provincial

government to bring the Mercy Ship to a coastal area called Lazaro Cardenas, overlooked by other relief organizations centered on Mexico City. I
flew into the port city of Acapulco to see what we might do. And that's
where the *Anastasis* first became a true hospital ship.

I drove north to Lazaro Cardenas, the on-land site nearest the earthquake epicenter just offshore. Houses were down everywhere, grain eleva-
tors damaged, buildings crushed, and the hospital for the poor built by
the Swiss government several years earlier had been severely damaged.
First-aid treatment was obviously needed, but so was every sort of medical treatment, including surgery. Our medical team was already working
in the town's general hospital, which was available for patients who could
afford to pay for their medical services. One of our first medical volunteers, a California surgeon named Dr. Gary Parker, had already performed
cleft lip and palate operations, a type of surgery previously unavailable yet
desperately needed in that rural area. *(see photo 4)*

"Isn't there anything you can do?" someone asked.

Yes, I remember thinking.

It was time.

The ship's holds were already filled with more than $2 million in
relief goods, including a $100,000 fire truck and, on a subsequent voyage,
an ambulance, and thousands of dollars' worth of medical equipment,
including a hospital X-ray machine and dental equipment. And now, the
Mercy Ship was also equipped with a new eye-surgery clinic.

So, while the volunteer crew built shelters and ran health clinics
on land, the medical team set up screenings for the first surgeries. The
Anastasis was about to become a fully functioning hospital ship. Medical
care would no longer be an afterthought of the charity; it was going to be
the primary focus—starting now.

When the government officials heard what I thought the *Anastasis*
was capable of doing, they began broadcasting from the state-controlled
radio stations about the Mercy Ship coming their way—letting their
people know we were ready, willing, and able to do free surgeries. They
only had to come. And they did.

Can you imagine how they must have felt, trusting their health to
strangers on a ship? Suffering makes you brave, I believe. And the very
bravest, the very first patient, was Señora Refugio Camacho, a sixty-eight-
year-old woman, eyes cloudy with cataracts, hobbling along on the arm

of her daughter. The team who were on hand to help Dr. Bob Dyer was a fittingly international one—a local Mexican anesthesiologist, a surgical nurse from South Africa, doctors from New Zealand and California, as well as a remarkable New Zealand woman named Simonne McCluskey, who would eventually marry the eye surgeon and become my replacement as the *Anastasis'* executive director. The next morning, I don't mind admitting that tears came to my eyes when Señora Camacho grabbed Dr. Dyer's hand and said: "Yo puedo ver!"

I can see!

In the following weeks, patients ranging from babies to great-grandmothers came onboard the big hospital ship sightless, and left seeing the world in all its glory. From cataract removal to correction of crossed eyes, the medical team gave the gift of sight to them all. None of us ever tired of witnessing those first hesitant moments as the bandages come off and the patient's brain begins to process the gift of sight.

When I think back, though, one special story does come to mind. We had a family travel to find us—the Tellez family. The couple had twelve children, four who were blind from birth because of congenital cataracts. When Señor Tellez heard the government's radio announcement of free eye surgeries, he put his four blind children in a little motorized dugout canoe and traveled down the Rio Balsas to Lazaro Cardenas. Then he led his children out of the canoe onto a public bus and made his way to the port, leading them all up the ship's gangway. They were a sight to behold. This is the image I will forever see: the children, from eldest to youngest, lined up behind the other, hand to hand, Señor Tellez in the lead, all in step, slowly making their way onto the Mercy Ship.

But as fascinating as that image was, nothing can compare to watching a child see for the very first time. I had the privilege of witnessing it on that day and on many days since. We take our sight so much for granted that it's hard to grasp how amazing the moment is when the brain signals the miracle of sight. For those like the Tellez children, born blind with cataracts, the optic nerve has never been damaged. But since this is the first time in their lives their brains have been called on to translate images through their eyes, the process does not happen instantly. And if you're privileged to witness such a drama, you notice the same distinct, dramatic pause as the brain registers the incoming images for the first time. You first see it in their faces—the surprise, the joy, the wonder—and then, finally, you see it in their eyes.

And when the patient is a child, the next few seconds are even more unforgettable. Bandages are removed from the child's eyes, and immediately the eyes begin to search for the child's mother. Every blind child knows his or her mother by the sound of her voice. And when the child hears that voice and sees his or her mother for the very first time, it is something to behold.

I'll never forget the first time I noticed a mother on the stern deck, holding her little boy and pointing all around at the big, colorful world. "That's the sky, and that color is blue," I could hear her telling him. "And that is the ocean. Now you know how beautiful it is."

It is said that eyes are the windows of the soul.

Of the sixty million blind people in the world, 50 percent could see with a twenty-minute ambulatory surgery much like the ones we did on this very first hospital ship port visit. In the years ahead, a Mercy Ship designed specifically to be a floating eye hospital would serve the entire Caribbean, specializing in the wonderful medical field of giving back the gift of sight. Eye surgery and care is already a Mercy Ships cornerstone, and, in a way, I can't help but believe it has something to do with these first successes.

Here, in this small port on the edge of the Mexican coast, after ten long years, the Mercy Ship *Anastasis* finally fulfilled her destiny. She was now a hospital ship.

So now I got down to business. We began establishing relationships with governments. In the next few months as we sailed the Mercy Ship around the Caribbean, we prepared our first protocol, a legal document we signed for our host governments, which described our potential and intent under their auspices. Our sailing year would center around spending months at a time performing surgeries in needy ports upon invitation, then sailing back to European or U.S. harbors for repairs, recruitment, and fund-raising in order to turn around, sail back, and perform surgeries for the world's poor once again.

In the next few months, while we solidified such full-time hospital ship plans and made Caribbean port visits and U.S. maintenance stops, we also aided relief efforts in the wake of Hurricane Gilbert, and later, as we toured the U.S. east coast, we docked with the *Good Samaritan* in Washington, D.C., where we met as many U.S. government officials as we could.

Finally it was time to go where Mercy Ships had been destined to go since the first tactical plans developed in Switzerland a decade earlier . . . Africa. The way to get to Africa was via Europe.

On May 3, 1990, the Mercy Ship left New London, Connecticut, bound for Europe. It would be the first crossing of the Atlantic since our first 1982 voyage.

But strangely enough, this was the moment that Deyon and I decided to move off the ship, our family's home for a decade. And that decision would change the course of Mercy Ships in ways I could never have imagined.

LIFE BOAT

by John Dyson, excerpted from *Reader's Digest,*
U.S.A., June 2002

Dateline: Cotonou, Benin
6°21' N, 2°23' E

A slim, rangy figure with short-cut hair and three gold bars on the shoulder tabs of his white shirt pauses on the gangway of the Anastasis. *He gazes for a moment at the cluttered, chaotic, dilapidated port city, takes a deep breath and braces himself for the tough job ahead . . . Dr. Gary Parker goes ashore and drives to a nearby sports arena. Outside, some 3,000 are standing, sitting, lying in the steamy equatorial heat. Waiting. For him. The maxillofacial surgeon may be their last hope . . . (see photo 4)*

Angelle Koffi cooked meals to sell by the roadside. But her customers were few. People thought she was cursed, and they turned away from her. A tumor as large as a mango grew out of Angelle's cheek, distorting her nose and mouth sideways . . . Shunned, the 24-year-old orphan slept in an isolated hut. On the street, people ran at the sight of her . . . only at church did she find some hope. One day, a visitor brought exciting news: "The white ship is coming!"

Once in the stadium, Dr. Gary Parker begins to look for good prospects for surgery. The UCLA-trained surgeon still has to turn away one in three who are too weak with advanced diseases to survive an operation . . . Near the end of the day, a slim woman with a bowed head approaches him with a shawl covering her face. Parker tenderly folds back the cloth over Angelle's face. Her tumor is operable; he selects her for surgery.

"Welcome to Mercy Ships," a nurse says to a hesitant Angelle, taking her hand. After a grueling ten-hour surgery, she awakes fearful, her face stiff and heavy. A nurse put a mirror in her hand. There were bandages, stitches, and enormous swelling. But there was no tumor. All day she inspected her face. When Dr. Parker comes to visit, she takes

his hand in both of hers. "I can give you nothing but my thanks," she says through an interpreter, and her lopsided grin lights up the ship . . .

One day, months later, a confident young woman walked gracefully down the gangway. In the pocket of her blue frock was a document that explained why the picture on her ID card no longer matched her face. When she got home, her pastor embraced her, whirling her round. "Angelle, you are beautiful now!' he said. As Gary Parker was deftly sewing up an infant's cleft palate, a nurse told him about Angelle's welcome at home. "That's why we're in business," he said, smiling broadly. "Angelle has got her life back."

SHIP'S LOG:
1989–1991

● ● ●

Garden Valley, Texas
32°21' N, 95°23' W

Lomé, Togo
6°10' N, 01°21' E

Tema, Ghana
05°37' N, 00°01' W

CHAPTER 7

FINALLY TO AFRICA

We must use time wisely and forever realize that the time is always right to do right.

—Nelson Mandela

"You're moving where?"

If there was ever a bad time to move off the ship, this moment—on the eve of fulfilling the Mercy Ships floating hospital vision—would surely be it.

Yet that is exactly what happened. And no one was more surprised than I was. After living for ten years onboard the *Anastasis*, Deyon and I moved our four children off the ship. Why would we choose now, of all times, to move off the ship? The answer had to do with J. P., our handicapped son.

My life with Mercy Ships, I have noticed, has fallen into ten-year segments.

The first decade was spent living in an international city in the heart of Europe, letting the Mercy Ships vision form.

The next ten years were pioneering years for Mercy Ships, full of trials and errors.

The following decade I had always envisioned as time spent building Mercy Ships' infrastructure. That's exactly what happened, just not exactly as I'd planned or from where I planned it. And I was about to learn why. It would be the next in a series of lessons taught by my son.

How do we measure the value of a life? J. P. cannot speak, and yet just as Mother Teresa said so many years before, what we learned in caring for, loving, and providing for him had translated into the Mercy Ships vision. J. P. continued to remind us each and every day of the value of the individual life and the God-given right to its quality. And once again, our son was telling us the way that Mercy Ships should go.

I just had to listen.

In 1989, John Paul, then thirteen, was very frustrated with life on the ship. Finally, the teachers at the onboard school came to us. They didn't say he was uneducable, but as politely as they could, they let us know something had to give. I remember looking at his special chair the teachers had brought into the kindergarten class where J. P. had gone every day for years, thinking how big it was in comparison to all the others, and I realized what was not being said. Being so big, he was no doubt more than a little frightening to some of the smaller children in the class.

To better care for J. P., it was time to move on.

The move was common sense, of course, and Deyon saw it clearly, but I took a little longer. I was involved in the ship at the deepest level of my soul. *How could I possibly leave the* Anastasis *at this point? This is my life. What will this mean for Mercy Ships?* Or that's what I was thinking, what I couldn't say out loud. Even the greatest ideas can flourish or falter on just such decisions. It took me quite a while to process it, but moving ashore turned out to be not only the right decision, but a pivotal one. Leaving the ship was exactly what I needed to do, not only for J. P., but for the future of Mercy Ships. I had been trying to grow the charity from onboard. And if I had stayed on the ship, Mercy Ships probably would have remained a small operation, limited in size and scope. And truthfully, I doubt if it would still be in existence today.

Where did we move? As strange as it may sound, we moved a ship-based charity to deep in the heart of landlocked East Texas.

After our decision, I had gone ahead of the *Anastasis* to Europe in order to gain advice from old friends on where we should move. I had a list for our move of things "Required" on one side and things "Desired" on the other side. And under "Required," we had listed the most seemingly obvious need—a port location. We had outgrown our resource office facilities in Los Angeles, the most logical option. While we were considering all that, we were offered property in the Texas heartland—an eventual four hundred acres in rural East Texas with an amazing amount of amenities for what we wanted to do. The only problem was that it happened to be hundreds of miles from the sea. So we set the idea aside and kept looking.

And that's when Henri André and his Swiss Atlantic experts once again entered the Mercy Ships story. "If we can run a fleet of ships out of Switzerland, which will never have a port, you can do the same," they said. All we truly needed was access to a good airport and telecommunications. So in September of 1989, we moved "port location" from "Required" to "Desired," and ultimately found ourselves saying yes to the spacious acreage with all its extras, hundreds of acres, more than 250 miles from the gulf and almost one hundred miles from the nearest international airport. It was the perfect place for a charity organization focused on ships—perfectly improbable, that is. But that was exactly what we had come to expect from this Mercy Ships journey of ours.

In early fall 1989, we moved to the rolling hills of East Texas, and that has been our headquarters and our home ever since—a place where J. P. has the space he needs and deserves, and where Mercy Ships has the space to grow. We settled in and began to plot and plan the future.

The fact that we were sending the *Anastasis* back to Europe in preparation for Africa required deepened relationships with as many countries as possible. So we studied our strategic plan once again and got to work developing legal and physical presences in seaport countries; rethinking the way we governed and managed work; and most important, forming an international board so that each of the nations where we opened support and resource offices would feel Mercy Ships was theirs as well as ours.

I had to let go and trust. What I have learned about authority is that the more you give away, the more you have. The more you try to keep, the more you lose. If the idea is the right one, then there's room for everyone. In other words, it was time to move from the bootstrap mentality, so important in the beginning, to the attitude that could take us to the next level—to a true global presence with potential as big as the sea itself.

I sensed a deep need to make myself more accountable. I had always had a legal board, but now that wasn't enough. If Mercy Ships was going to grow, I needed the wisdom and expertise of independent and knowledgeable individuals from all walks of life. We were already a floating global community of nations in so many ways, but to involve the rest of the world community meant thinking in new ways and persuading new thinkers to catch the Mercy Ships vision. We had the potential to encompass the best of all charity worlds—traditional, faith-based, humanitarian, corporate, and governmental—if we did this right. So I began to ask for help from some of the best minds in the world, captains of industry and medicine and commerce and diplomacy as well as captains of ocean-going ships—and I got it.

A group of these experts believed so deeply in Mercy Ships' global potential that they offered services far beyond my wildest hopes. Four men in particular worked closely with us, bringing the remarkable global expertise needed to fit our vision—William S. Kanaga, chairman of Arthur Young (now Ernst & Young) worldwide accounting firm, chairman of the U.S. Chamber of Commerce, and chairman of the Center for International Private Enterprise; William C. Turner, former ambassador to the Organization for Economic Cooperation and Development (OECD); Myron E. Ullman (Mike), a former White House Fellow, whose international business experience would soon extend around the globe—in Asia (the Wharf Holdings), the U.S. (R. H. Macy & Co., J. C. Penney, and DFS Group, Ltd.), and in Europe (LVMH Moët Hennessy Louis Vuitton); and Lord Ian McColl, professor of surgery at Guy's Hospital.

They oversaw the structural, internal changes and provided the network of accountability needed to produce the future we all desired. Along with their unparalleled business acumen just when we needed it the most, they also brought hearts to serve the world's poor. The transformation they designed for Mercy Ships was amazing to watch.

Soon we restructured into a legal multinational charity, beginning in Norway, Sweden, Denmark, Germany, Holland, Switzerland, and France. By the turn of the century, Mercy Ships would be a legal entity on five continents of the world. And all of it began when we moved ashore and began thinking like the global entity we wanted to be.

In the years to come, former British Prime Minister John Major would dedicate the International Support Center, taking the long drive into the springtime Texas countryside to say memorable and warm words about our landlocked ship headquarters: "It is from here in East Texas that medical and logistical supplies are organized and vessels dispatched. It is from here in East Texas that the healing flows."

The move to Garden Valley, Texas, had been a risk. As usual, though, my friend Henri André had been right. By April 1990, with my family settling into life on solid ground and our organizational staff working from national offices around the world, the *Anastasis* set sail across the Atlantic toward Europe. I flew ahead to finish preparing the way.

The feel of history in the making seemed to be everywhere during that pre-Africa tour of Europe, one for the world history books, one for the Mercy Ships history books, and one for my own family history book. In June 1990, in the peaceful harbor of Kristiansand, Norway, as the Mercy Ship opened her doors, I felt the eyes of my Norwegian shipbuilding ancestors take a good look at this ship and this mountain-reared descendant of theirs. Then in July, we visited Poland.

The Berlin Wall had just come down, guards had abandoned Checkpoint Charlie, and Poland had its first free elections since World War II, beginning its historic transition from communism to a democratic society. And we wanted to do our small part to help. The *Anastasis* unloaded more than a million dollars of donations, including modern eye surgery equipment earmarked for the Gdansk hospital. Working double shifts, Solidarity longshoremen labored with the ship's crew to unload the donations. And the Mercy Ship was in port on the day the shipyard workers brought down the huge bronze statue of "Mother Russia" a few blocks away. Officials made speeches, and, in a fitting and memorable gesture, one man actually stepped forward and tweaked the statue's nose, to the crowd's applause.

In August, after a month in Rotterdam, the ship passed Lloyd's Register annual surveys.

We were good to go.

So we sailed to London, where we held medical receptions onboard, inviting health care professionals to visit the Mercy Ship in the hopes of recruiting their hands and their hearts to bring hope and healing to the poor.

One of the men who walked up the gangway was Sir John Chalstry. "I am fascinated with what you do, and I believe in what you are doing and how you are doing it," he said. "I may soon have the opportunity to be the Lord Mayor of the city of London, and part of my charge will be to use the prestige of the office to help two charities of choice. My first choice will be St. John's Ambulance. The second charity is not selected. I would like to suggest that you consider me making you the second charity. If you agree, we could use the Mansion House in London for a black-tie dinner to help make the charity known in the U.K."

I, of course, quickly agreed.

True to his word, Sir John Chalstry became Lord Mayor of London soon after, and we became his second "charity of choice." And just like that, we were propelled into the English public eye. The public awareness, as well as the medical and financial partnerships that came from his support, would fuel the next pivotal decade for Mercy Ships in ways we could never have imagined that night before we sailed to Africa.

While in Europe during that preparation time, over sixty-five thousand people visited the Mercy Ship. And as donations came in, we excitedly loaded the materials onboard for our first extended visit to Africa. We were ready for a whole new set of challenges—or we thought we were. As usual, no matter how much you think you are prepared, something unexpected always happens.

Our first stop was going to be Ghana. The plan was to stay several months. Our long-range goal was to spend longer and longer times each year serving both French and English-speaking Africa, all the way from Senegal in the north to Madagascar around the Cape. So, for this first big outing, we had chosen Ghana very deliberately to help our chances of success. We had all of our "ducks in a row" strategically, for Ghana. The need had been assessed. It was an English-speaking country. It was economically stable. We even had former Mercy Ships staff who'd moved back there, which meant we had a local partner within the nation to help. We had met with the minister of health; we had been invited; all the right documents were signed and sealed; and we were ready, able, and willing to deliver.

But three weeks before departure, while docked in Denmark, we were in for a surprise.

I'll never forget the moment. We were in the middle of our government and civic reception in Copenhagen onboard the ship. I had just met the Ghanaian Consul General when he leaned near and said, "I need to speak with you." I led him to my office and closed the door.

He told me that the head of state in Ghana had just contacted him, and the decision to invite us had been "frozen."

I looked at him strangely. "Frozen?"

"That is diplomatic parlance for 'you can't come to Ghana,'" he explained.

I couldn't find my voice for a few seconds. Finally, I said, "Mr. Consul General, we've put in two years of advance work. We have invested in surveys of health care needs; we are partnering with the ministry of health. We have it all organized, and we're only three weeks to departure. What do I do?"

His advice was to the point: First, go to another nation. Second, don't beg. "If you come back to Ghana with your hat in hand, you will never get into any African nation," he said. Then he added, "There will be an answer."

I don't know how long I sat there after the consul general left.

I should have been thinking about alternate plans, about how to explain this to donors and our new board and staff. And I especially should have been thinking about where to go from here, considering I had no contacts in Africa other than Ghana. But, instead, I was suddenly reminded that Mercy Ships did not belong to me. I remember that being the one clear thought, a reflection from out of nowhere, in the long minutes after the consul general dropped his bombshell.

And as I was thinking about Mercy Ships in that broad and sweeping way, a Swiss friend's name came to mind—Daniel Schaerer. Daniel once told me about his family, and I remembered that an uncle, a Dr. DeLord, had been a French medical missionary in Togo. Jacques produced the first Kabile language grammar, translating parts of the New Testament into Kabile. Future president Gnassingbe Eyadema was a son of this tribe. So I dialed Daniel Schaerer, told him the situation, and mentioned I remembered his uncle.

He said, "Don, it's interesting you should call and mention this, especially now. My uncle just returned from Togo." The current head of state, President Gnassingbe Eyadema, had just flown him first-class Air France to Togo, rolled out the red carpet—literally—to honor him for his educational service to the Togolese people so many years ago. While there, President Eyadema asked him, "Are there people like you in the world today who would do what you did for the people of Togo?"

"Well," Daniel's uncle had said, "my nephew knows a group."

I didn't have time to think about how unusual that was at the time. I had a big problem to solve. So I leveled with Daniel: "Would you mind asking your uncle to call the president back to see if he'd like that group to come—and come right now?"

Daniel agreed, and in no time, it seemed, he had phoned back to report that his uncle had phoned President Eyadema, explained that Ghana had frozen its invitation to the group he'd mentioned, so would Togo open the port for them to come instead?

President Eyadema's response? A resounding *yes!*

And so, the *Anastasis* sailed as planned three weeks from that day. But it sailed not Ghana, but to Togo.

Along the coast, tiny sea villages dotted the shoreline along the western edge of the African continent. It was a view that had barely changed in centuries. When we arrived in Lomé, tugs swung the Mercy Ship portside to the dock, and we quickly arranged our first screening day, putting up announcements in clinics, churches, and government agencies, to help spread the word that a floating hospital was offering free medical services. All they had to do was come. And they did. We were quickly in business.

After operating only two or three weeks, some of our new friends came to warn us about what they had heard: "The Ghanaian secret police are coming to the ship. They can't believe what you are doing."

The port in Togo was only thirty minutes from the Ghana/Togo border, such as it is. Togo and Ghana are neighboring nations. The French and the British had split the land along West Africa's Gold Coast during colonization, dividing the land into two countries, but the boundary line doesn't exist for the Ewe people, one of the tribal affiliations of both populations. They move back and forth across the border as they've done for centuries, and so word travels back and forth with them. Obviously, Ghana's government officials had begun to hear about what we were doing. And now, it seemed, someone had sent their secret police to investigate. This did not sound good.

But yet again, we were in for a surprise.

"We made a mistake," one of the police said. "Would you cancel what you are doing in Togo and come to Ghana as you originally planned?"

We said no, that we had made a commitment and were going to stick to it. However, we did say that we would come to them next. And after our time in Togo ended in February, we sailed to Ghana and stayed for three months.

After a while, we discovered the reason Ghana froze our invitation. Rumors had reached each of the Ghanaian embassies in Europe that the

Mercy Ship coming their way was really full of terrorists in surgeons' clothes, that we had AK-47s in our cargo holds and that when our gangway went down, like the Trojan Horse of Troy, enemy insurgents would rush into the country to stage a coup d'état. Of course, that panicked the nation of Ghana. They didn't know us. No one in Africa knew us yet.

That could have been the end of that story, but instead, we had a very important visitor near the end of our stay. We were only hours from sailing. All of a sudden, we heard a flurry of activity on the dock. Several military jeeps pulled up to our gangway. From one of them stepped the Ghanaian head of state, President Jerry Rawlins.

Our captain met him at the gangway and took the president to the hospital. He asked to see the ship, so he was taken to the hospital, where our surgeon, Dr. Gary Parker, was finishing his examination of a cleft-lip-and-palate patient. The small boy was returning for one last postoperative follow-up. On the wall behind the boy, near where his father stood, were "before" and "after" snapshots of him.

Studying the photos, President Rawlins asked the little boy, "This was you?" The boy nodded happily. The president wanted to hear the whole story—what it was like to have surgery on the ship, how many other successful surgeries they'd seen, and on and on. Finally, after hearing all the father and son had to say, President Rawlins said to the captain, "Would you assemble the remaining crew? I want to speak to them."

The members of the crew assembled in the large meeting room onboard . . . President Rawlins stepped to the microphone and said, "I am here to apologize. I am the one who canceled your invitation. I didn't believe people like you existed today. It was too good to be true. Now that I realize so many more of my countrymen could have been helped had I not made that decision, I feel I need to apologize to you." He did not have to say that to us. The gesture spoke of the integrity of the man. His visit was a fitting and special end to a very strange beginning for Mercy Ships' Africa era.

On April 12, 1991, the big Mercy Ship turned and sailed back toward Europe, and that turn was also a literal turning point for us all. Togo and Ghana proved the floating-hospital concept was the right one. The center of the Mercy Ships' universe was now irrevocably its medical heart. This was our future, and West Africa's neediest countries would soon become the true home of the Mercy Ship *Anastasis.*

DOCUMENTARIES & ARTS: AFRICAN ER

Excerpt, BBC.com for BBC-TV
Documentary *Broadcast date: January 31, 2004*

Thousands of people have trekked hundreds of miles—sometimes from other countries—to the port of Freetown, Sierra Leone, just to find out if they are one of the lucky ones who will be picked to have their lives changed. This gathering of the country's outcasts is of biblical proportions. But it's not "African Pop Idol." People with terrible disfigurements, facial tumours the size of footballs, club feet, incontinence and blindness have turned up, desperate for surgery aboard a floating hospital . . .

Our presenter, Tash Monie, a glamorous south London girl who has never seen anything like this, watches as the volunteer nurses and doctors make the tough decisions about who should get treatment and who won't. It's an exhausting, heart-wrenching day. How do you decide who gets picked? And what does it feel like turning people away?

For Tash, the "African ER" experience has just started. And it's going to be one [heck] of an experience. She plunges in at the deep end after she arrives in war-ravaged Sierra Leone—handing out water to the waiting crowds and hearing their desperate stories . . .

SHIP'S LOG:
1991–2004

● ● ●

Puerto Cortes, Honduras
15°51' N, 87°57' W

Abidjan, Ivory Coast
05°18' N, 04°00' W

Suva, Fiji
18°08' S, 178°26' E

Dakar, Senegal
14°40' N, 17°22' W

Tamatave, Madagascar
18°09' S, 49°25' E

CHAPTER 8

BRINGING HOPE AND HEALING

No one would remember the Good Samaritan if he only had good intentions.

—Margaret Thatcher

Of all the memories I have of those first hospital ship visits, the most vivid is the sight of people waiting in line during a screening day. Even now, after all these years, the sight is still incredibly moving. It is the moment we have been working toward for months. It is why we sail. Advance teams have gone ahead of the ship to advertise the medical screenings and the type of surgeries done onboard, hanging posters in health clinics and partnering with governmental, charitable, and religious organizations to spread the word.

People have come from all over the country, many traveling for days and sleeping overnight, hoping to secure a place near the front of the queue. As the word has spread through the years, the crowds have swelled to the point that government agencies have begun to open stadiums and sports arenas to hold the thousands who come and wait.

After the successful visits to Togo and Ghana, Mercy Ships received invitations from more than a dozen nations. We have now sailed to places with names rarely heard in the developed world, places such as New Caledonia, Barahona, Lomé, Conakry, Cotonou, Dakar, and Noumea. Needless to say, they are not tourist spots. They're not easily accessible and are rarely in the headlines for any reason other than poverty and strife. Few of them are on our mental maps of the world, but each is forever on the heart-maps of Mercy Ships crews.

Months of preparation were behind our first choice, and we quickly learned that it should always take that long. So, after that important first voyage, we tweaked our "grid," a checklist to help our destination decisions go along with the official protocol I'd initiated after our first Mexico hospital ship operation. We had already decided we would go only to a country that invited us. So a written invitation from the country's government had to begin the process.

Next, we evaluated the depth of medical needs within the nation. We were committed to going to the very poorest of the poor—countries in the lowest one-third of the neediest nations in the world, as published by the United Nations Annual Human Development Index. Haiti is in the poorest tier, for instance, as are Sierra Leone and Liberia.

Next the technical questions must be answered. Is the harbor deep enough? Are there enough berths so we won't interfere with commercial shipping? Can they provide garbage disposal? Do they have enough fresh water to meet our need for one hundred tons a day? Will the port authorities waive fees?

After that comes a risk analysis. How stable is the country? How good is the port security? Is the nation on the verge of anarchy or revolution? We check with both the U.S. State Department and the British Foreign Service for the latest information on any potential destination.

Then we meet with the minister of health and other health authorities to see if they will grant permission to the ship's medical staff to provide the surgeries, make visits to clinics, and undertake community health training. If permission is granted, then our various assessment teams—medical, dental, construction, water and sanitation, church and community health training—visit the port and surrounding villages.

When all of this is completed, the proposed port is presented to the Mercy Ships board and senior management, the final decision is made, we respond to the nation, and we put it on the schedule.

And all of that effort is to make this special day happen each year—the day we sail a Mercy Ship into a country, lower the gangway, and step ashore to begin offering hope and healing however we can.

Of course, it's one thing for a government to trust you. It's another to be an ordinary citizen who has seen none of our official assurances. Africans had every right to be wary of ships docking at their ports with offers too good to be true. Not only were we battling the slave ship horrors of the past, we were also battling their specters in the present. Each year, all along the sub-Saharan coastline, we hear rumors of a modern-day slave-labor ship that promises jobs and better lives to children, but that in reality offers forced labor and prostitution rings. Only word of mouth, straight from those helped and healed, could truly build trust in Mercy Ships. And that is exactly what happened. Soon people streamed into these port cities to wait in long lines for a chance to gain a surgical appointment card and the transformations those cards promised.

Medical screenings are a time when nearly the entire ship's crew gets involved by giving water, testing blood, checking temperatures, writing health histories, and escorting patients to the areas where doctors are examining people one by one. Most screening days can be as tragic as hopeful. Our Mercy Ships doctors have no choice but to turn away many patients we see because their diseases are too far advanced for us to help. All those who come are desperate and at their most vulnerable, and we strive to be worthy of their fragile trust. We have been so touched by some of the cases that we have set up a hospice branch to help support terminal cases during the months we are docked in port. The days ahead, the surgeries performed, and the life transformations they'll offer keep the team working, one by one, through the heartrending crowd and down the long screening line.

A hospital ship lends itself to certain areas of expertise, and those are the ones we embraced—maxillofacial surgery, plastic surgery, orthopedic surgery, eye surgery, and most recently, a specialty called vesicovaginal fistula (VVF) repair for women. *(see photos 5 and 6)* The stories that introduce each chapter of this book are examples of these specialties. The newborn Adam saved by the student Reginald was a cleft-lip-and-palate surgery. Señora Camacho received a cataract surgery, and Mariama's son Ansu, whose knee was wounded by a rebel soldier's bullet, was an orthopedic surgery. Edoh's need was for a maxillofacial surgery to remove her facial tumor.

All such stories have the power to break our hearts. But the power to change the endings of some is powerful medicine. Perhaps the best way to truly share the experience of a screening day is to tell one of these stories in depth.

Edoh's story is a perfect mirror for the drama of screening day for all concerned—and a great story. She came, literally tossed to us. What happened that day in Togo during the long screening day is a powerful story of mercy through the hands of gifted surgeons, but also the mercy extended by her crowd of fellow sufferers.

Her parents had all but given her up for dead when they heard about the hospital ship's return to their country. The tumor on the side of their daughter's face was the size of a grapefruit and was slowly, relentlessly closing off her airway. Her parents traveled five hundred kilometers to bring her to the dock of Togo's port city, Lomé. By the time they arrived with Edoh, the line was heartbreakingly long, and Edoh was gasping for breath. Her father, in desperation, lifted her above his head, and someone beside him took her and passed her to the head of the line. *(see photos 2 and 3)*

I have always been amazed at the inner calm of most Africans, even those in the direst distress. Our experience with screening day waiting lines is usually one of orderly quiet with hope in the air. That day the crowds were larger than we expected. In the five years since we last visited Togo, word had spread so far and wide that the city's officials and we were caught unprepared for the crush.

The long line that snaked back into the city had become a massive crowd. And as the crowd was pressing dangerously up against the dock's fencing, around which we had directed the line for the screening tests, we were forced to close the iron gates momentarily for crowd control. But then one of our security crew saw a child with a grotesque facial tumor being passed toward the front, above the crowd, person to person, hand to hand, and could hear her desperate gasps for breath.

Everyone in that line was suffering beyond anything most people in the Western world can fathom, and yet these people instantly saw a child in an even more desperate, immediate need of help. And as the crowd continued to be pushed against the fence between the screening area and the line, one by one those hands moved little Edoh to the front and then over the fence into the waiting arms of Jon Syrbe, a Mercy Ships crew member.

What made this even more poignant was that Jon had been born with a cleft lip and palate, endured nine operations in his young life, and had recently undergone further corrective surgery onboard. John took one look at Edoh, heard her gasps, and rushed her to the surgeons, who performed a tracheotomy. In the months ahead, Edoh underwent a series of operations, including one in Germany, to correct the damage done by the tumor. Then one day, right before we sailed, she went home with her parents to grow up like any other normal African child.

Edoh's medical problem is not uncommon in West Africa. Mercy Ships has performed many of these operations to remove jaw tumors, saving countless people from suffocation, starvation, and death. But such deformities occasionally hold more suffering than just potential death. If you have a physical deformity, you not only have little hope for the future, but you are usually an outcast. In some remote villages, stories are told of midwives snatching newborn babies with cleft lips and palates and burying them alive. In others, the family shuns mother and baby, because they believe the devil has touched them both.

Many people in the developing world live daily with the fear of a curse being put on them. And such deformities are, more often than not, seen as the result of such curses. Those who have such a condition have little hope. They can't be educated, few people will employ them, and people often run from or even throw stones at them. They are left to a life of begging or, worse, a life lived in the shadows of the only civilization they've ever known. They become a nonperson, hiding in the bush, shunned, literally waiting to die.

We've learned to leave time for a second screening, because only after news of dramatic success stories filter back into the villages do many with the worst disfigurements have the courage to come out of hiding. The doctors who volunteer from around the world are often surprised when patients wince or shrink away as they reach to examine them. The patients do not draw back from fear of physical pain, but because that moment is often the first time in years another human has dared to touch them.

After the screening schedule has been filled, in the coming weeks people just like Edoh will fill the beds of the ship's recovery wards. Most of their faces will be swollen, bruised, and bandaged—but without fail, on the first early-morning rounds the next day, most of them will borrow mirrors to admire themselves. When they see the medical staff, they turn their heads and flex their new smiles. I'll never forget the first time I saw a mother holding her little boy, who could now see again, standing at the ship's stern, showing him the world. It was the same amazing moment as I'd been privileged to witness in Mexico, but now it was happening on the other side of the world.

And as the wards fill up during the months we're in port, we get to know these people very well and often become very close to them.

But it's not that way when we first meet them on screening day. The hope and pain in the eyes of most of those in line is nearly always mingled with a touch of fear.

"What do we have to do?" is a constant question.

"Nothing," we say. "There is no catch. Everything is free. We treat everyone without regard to race, religion, sex, or creed."

This is delicate territory. We are serving the most vulnerable of the vulnerable. Who wouldn't say anything to be healed of one's horrible suffering? And who wouldn't find it hard to believe such a gift comes without one string attached? But that's the beauty of Mercy Ships. Offering the gift of health in any context but sheer altruism and love has deep flaws. And so we go out of our way to be sensitive to the fears of those we screen, those people hoping against all hope to be able to receive such a gift.

Within days, though, everything has changed. The relationships we form with those who come onto a ship for medical help almost defy description. Let me try to describe it in another context. When you meet someone for the first time, there is a relationship timeline. You don't expect him or her to be considered a close, intimate family friend within the first several meetings. In some cultures that requires twenty years, so a person can have only so many of such deeply bonded relationships in a lifetime. And if you are an outsider who doesn't speak another person's language, who is not from the other person's culture, your attempts to have a close relationship with that person might take a lifetime to form, if it happens at all.

But when you sail into a port city and perform a life-changing surgery on a family member, all of that evaporates. Twenty years collapse into twenty-four hours. And all of a sudden, you are no longer an outsider. Instant bonding takes place. Barriers are down. So the Mercy Ships crew must tread very softly in the beginning, if we are truly doing what we say we are: putting love into action and offering medical care with no strings attached.

As time goes by, we often find ourselves explaining why we are there. Mercy Ships follows the 2000-year-old model of Jesus in bringing hope and healing. Some serve onboard because of their faith, putting their beliefs into everyday action; some serve because of their expertise, giving of their talents and gaining experience they could never find anywhere else in the civilized world. Some serve because they love the sea, and they want to experience a seafaring way that is not all about the bottom line—something worthy—wanting to make a lasting difference in the world.

"You mean you don't get paid to do this?" our patients often ask.

"No. We do it because of a deeper purpose," is my usual answer.

And actually, I think we aren't that unusual. I'm convinced that the desire for deeper purpose resides within everyone. It's built-in. We truly do want to help our neighbor if we have the chance. I've observed this dynamic in the inner cities of not only the United States but nations around the world, as well as the faraway places of sub-Saharan Africa, the Middle East, the South Pacific, and Asia—people doing a little bit for the next person, trying to make the world a better place, even if it's only in the tiniest of ways. The fellow sufferers who helped Edoh by lifting her over their heads despite their own pain are perhaps the best example of this impulse in us all.

A recent trends analyst described Mercy Ships as a nontraditional charity creating modern partnerships with individuals, corporations, churches, charities, and governments. Humans make up organizations, and the vast majority of humanity has this built-in desire to leave the world a better place—somehow, someway—if given the chance.

Interestingly enough, a funny thing happens when the built-in desire becomes action. For those poorest of the poor whose lives come in contact with a Mercy Ship, they never forget the day everything changed with the help of a surgeon's scalpel and hundreds of pairs of loving, ship-worthy hands. But it goes both ways. When you reach out to serve the poor, you discover it is they who give to you, not just the other way around. Their grace, patience, and gratitude in response to the smallest act of kindness changes those privileged to serve them.

Actions speak loudest on a Mercy Ship. A respect for others—wherever they are, whatever their culture—is a guiding tenet of every port visit, during screening day and throughout each individual's stay onboard. Armed with that respect and governmental invitations, all that is truly necessary for us to gain trust is a few testimonials from transformed relatives, friends, and neighbors dancing back down the ship's gangway.

And that's exactly what has happened.

THE STORY OF VVF WOMEN

Dateline: Lomé, Togo
6°10' N, 01°21' E

Akou had already given birth to children, but when another came along in 1996, she could not deliver him. For four days she labored—and, finally, with her son born dead, she no longer had control of her bladder. Her husband left her. She tried to make a living by selling goats, but people didn't like to come near her because of her smell. Her husband's other three wives shunned her, often laughing at her, pointing their fingers and making fun of her always-wet skirts. They believed she would die.

Millions of women live daily with the same humiliation and dejection. Often barren and with a stench that drives them to seclusion, they stay in the shadows, with no voice to speak out against their unjust suffering.

They suffer with vesicovaginal fistulas (VVFs), and experts estimate they number in the millions worldwide. When obstructed labor causes a fistula, or hole, to form between the bladder and vagina, women find the constant trickle of urine, and sometimes feces, makes normal life impossible. Women who have undergone VVF surgeries onboard a Mercy Ship also reveal other causes: rape at a young age, accidents, or the slip of a knife while having a Caesarean delivery. (see photos 5 and 6)

In a part of the world where a woman's worth lies in her ability to bear children and usefulness as a wife, these women are often abandoned. And so they suffer alone. Akou, too, thought she would die from her misery. But she didn't, and finally, after seven years of suffering, she danced down the gangway of the Mercy Ship, dry after her own successful surgery onboard.

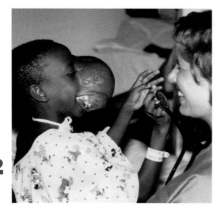

1] **SCREENING DAY** - On Screening Day, thousands wait patiently, hoping for a life-changing surgery.

2] **MEET EDOH** - Nine-year-old Edoh could barely eat due to the tumor that destroyed her nose and filled her mouth. The growth blocked her airway, threatening a slow and horrible death by suffocation.

3] **EDOH MAKES PLANS** - Dr. Gary Parker and Dr. Luer removed the tumor and created an eye socket, a roof for her mouth, and a new nose. Two more surgeries were later performed. Now a young woman, Edoh plans to become a nurse in order to help others.

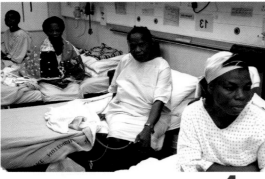

4

6

5

4] WOMAN'S WORTH - One of the most dangerous things that a West African woman can do is to give birth. Most births are not attended by skilled personnel. The West Africa Fistula Foundation estimates that between 2 and 3 million African women suffer from a serious childbirth injury (an obstetric fistula) that leaves them incontinent. In a society in which a woman's worth is based upon her ability to have children and in which physical problems receive little sympathy, these women are often rejected by family and friends.

5]   CELEBRATE - After corrective surgery, these women—wearing new dresses to symbolize new hope and a new life—celebrate with singing and dancing.

6] PROSPECTIVE PATIENT - Maxillofacial surgeon Dr. Gary Parker visits with a prospective patient. On Screening Day, Dr. Parker examines many patients to identify surgical candidates.

7

8

9

7] PATRICK THEN - Patrick lived with this tumor for over 15 years, enduring ridicule and rejection.

8] PATRICK NOW - Patrick had his first onboard surgery in 1992. He is now married, with children, and serves as the pastor of two mission churches in Sierra Leone.

9] CARIBBEAN MERCY - En route to South Korea and the Philippines, the *Caribbean Mercy* crew enjoyed spectacular scenery while navigating the Inside Passage in Alaska.

10

11

12

10] **SIDE-BY-SIDE** - The *Africa Mercy* and the *Anastasis* dock side-by-side in Monrovia, Liberia.

11] **MEETING THE PRESIDENT** - Mercy Ships President/Founder Don Stephens with the President of Benin, His Excellency Dr. Yayi Boni.

12] **MEET ABEL** - When Abel was a baby, his muscles stopped growing, but his bones did not. This caused his legs to bend backward at the knees, making him a target of ridicule from other children.

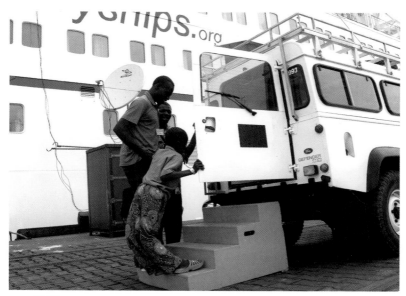

13

14

13] NOW ARRIVING - Abel arrives at the *Africa Mercy* for his life-transforming surgery.

14] ENJOYING NORMAL - After several surgeries onboard the *Africa Mercy*, 11-year-old Abel can walk normally and enjoy his favorite hobby...soccer.

15

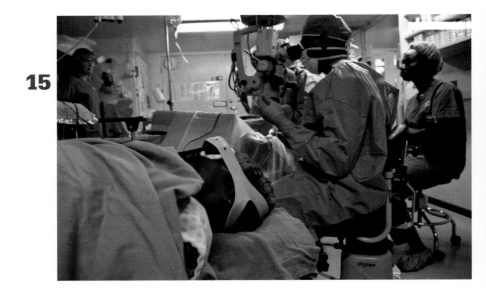

16

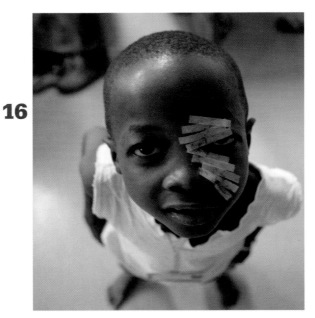

15] **CAPACITY BUILDING** - Mercy Ships increases health care capacity in West Africa by training local health care professionals.

16] **MAXILLOFACIAL** - Mercy Ships provides maxillofacial surgeries that remove tumors and repair cleft lips and palates.

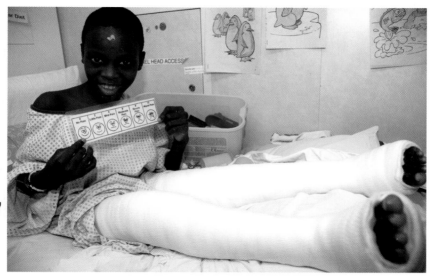

17

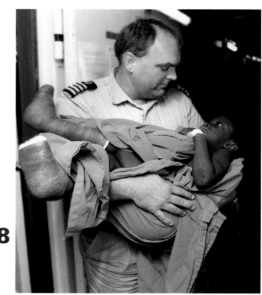

18

17] ORTHO CHANGES LIVES - Mercy Ships surgeons perform procedures to correct club feet, bowed legs, and other orthopedic conditions. As a result, children can run and play with their friends and have a normal life.

18] THE CARING CAPTAIN - Former Mercy Ships Captain Clem Ketchum carries a child from the surgery ward onboard one of our hospital ships.

19

19] OFFERING HOPE - Mercy Ships President/Founder Don Stephens enjoys a visit with a small patient.

SHIP'S LOG:
1990–2000

Cotonou, Benin
06°21' N, 02°23' E

Banjul, The Gambia
13°27' N, 16°35' W

Conakry, Guinea
9°30' N, 13°43' W

CHAPTER 9

HEART OF AFRICA

The true neighbor will risk his position, his prestige, and even his life for the welfare of others.

—Martin Luther King Jr.

"Don, I have a delegation down here from the United States. They would like to tour the ship," the gangway watchman informed me. "What should I do? The ship is closed on Sunday."

"Open the ship," I said. "I'll come down immediately."

Deyon and I had come to Togo with the board members. Once a year, our International Board travels to a ship to observe the life and work of a Mercy Ship in action. We had already been there five days, and we were leaving the next day. Most of the board members were visiting the city, but Deyon and I had chosen to stay onboard and rest. About 3 PM, the U.S. delegation appeared at the bottom of our gangway.

The group was in Togo as a part of a multinational group monitoring the Togo presidential elections, and while there had heard about a Mercy Ship docked in the port. They'd like to know more, they had told the crew member on watch.

So Deyon and I gave them a tour.

The group included the Togolese ambassador to the United States, Akoussoulelou Bodjona, U.S. Congresswoman Corrine Brown, and Martin Luther King III. Congresswoman Brown, upon her return to the States, introduced Mercy Ships to the black caucus of the U.S. House of Representatives for endorsement and support for what we are doing in Africa—a wonderful gesture. Martin Luther King III, president of the Southern Christian Leadership Council, was representing the SCLC as an official delegate observer of the election process.

It was an honor to meet them all. Meeting Martin Luther King Jr.'s son was not only a surprise, but an unusually significant moment for me. I have no idea what his thoughts were—if he knew he was embodying all the symbolism of his father's civil rights history, especially standing as we were on a ship docked along what once was Africa's slave coast. But as they left, I felt the weight of history surrounding me.

To work with the African continent is to be engaged with history almost every moment of the day. You can't help but face the past even as you work to heal old wounds as only hospital ships can.

As mentioned earlier, the rumors of slave ships were still very much alive along this coast, hundreds of years after slavery was abolished. They had grown to the point that in 2001 news spread around the world concerning a suspicious freighter believed to be just such a slave ship, carrying children away to forced labor or worse. A ship named the *Etireno* had become a "rogue" ship, having been turned away from Cameroon and Gabon, and was now being turned away from Benin as well. The rusting ship had docked within sight of the *Anastasis* there in Benin, before it was forced back to sea. News photographers and reporters touring the *Anastasis* during that week found themselves asking permission to shoot footage of the *Etireno* from our ship's top deck to feed to their home offices.

Child labor is common in parts of Africa, and child trafficking has long been known as an African problem. During that time, the United Nations estimated more than two hundred thousand children were working as slave laborers. The charges were never confirmed about the rogue ship, even though officials feared there was truth to the rumors, but global media including CBS, BBC, CNN, and major international newspapers carried stories of the suspicion around the world and back. That's how this dreaded chapter of the past lives on in this part of the world.

In 1999, Benin's President Kérékou became the first African leader to publicly apologize for African involvement in the slave trade, and soon afterward, Ghanaian President Jerry Rawlings offered an apology as well. Kérékou held a historic reconciliation conference to bring together the descendants of all those involved—from representatives of the historic slave cities to heads of state to descendants of slaves.

In 2000, the *Anastasis* visited The Gambia, the African country where Alex Haley's famous ancestor lived. I was one of the millions of people deeply affected by the literary phenomenon *Roots*, Alex Haley's chronicle of the tracing of his "roots" back through family legends to the African ancestor sold into slavery from the Gambia River. And the impact of that book was not only felt in the West. Africans are equally aware of the saga, especially Gambians.

George Haley, Alex Haley's brother, was the U.S. ambassador to his ancestral country in 2000, and we were privileged to meet him. Inside the ambassador's residence hung a huge mural of the Haley family tree, tracing those famous roots all the way back to the Gambian who was forced into slavery and sent by slave ship to America.

Ambassador Haley invited several of us to take a trip up the Gambia River in the U.S. Embassy's small boat to villages we wanted to visit inland. As we motored up the Gambia River, I could almost see the years recede. After only a few miles inland, the country looked as it must have looked two hundred years ago. Ambassador Haley, Dr. Gary Parker, and I discussed a lot of things on that trip, but one comment Ambassador Haley made deeply affected me in that special setting. As terrible as slavery was, I recall him saying, he couldn't help but wonder where he might be had his famous ancestor Kunte Kinte not been taken as a slave. Wasn't it amazing that a "seventh-generation son of a slave could come back to serve as ambassador to his ancestor's homeland?"

The *Anastasis*' executive director, Daslin Small, a Jamaican-born, Toronto-educated woman of African descent, has expressed the same full-circle feelings. The first time she sailed to Africa on a ship, she said her "heart choked up." Onboard with her were more than forty West Africans, along with hundreds of Europeans, Britons, and Americans. "Here I was," she said, "the descendant of Africans sold onto slave ships, leading a crew of descendants of both slaves and slavers on a ship of healing back to Africa."

During that trip down the Gambia River with Ambassador Haley, we met the village elders of Brikama who wanted to know about our hospital ship, about the surgeries and the community development projects we'd begun to do on land. It was the first time Mercy Ships had been to The Gambia. They didn't know us, and we didn't know them. I did know, however, that the city elders were Muslim. I also knew many of the parents had been afraid to bring their children to the medical screenings near the hospital ship because of the modern-day slave ship rumors. I could only imagine what they were thinking.

What do they want to hear? I wondered. *What is the most important thing I could say to them?*

In this land where history is mostly passed on by word of mouth, I knew these leaders could tell me which tribes were raided and which tribes participated with the Europeans in the slave raids centuries ago. So, with the help of Dr. Schneider, who spoke the local language of Mandinka fluently, I decided to talk about our common history: "Ships have many purposes in history, some good and some bad. You know that ships have come to this river before, and your people have been abused. But I represent ships that are totally different. They are not slave ships but ships of hope. Not ships of aggression and abuse, but ships that bring healing. We are here wanting to partner with you. We want long-term relationships based on mutual trust."

At the end of our presentation, the Muslim tribal chieftains asked, "Could we pray together before we finish this meeting?"

Taken aback, I quickly agreed.

They said, "Here is how we want to do it, to recognize our mutuality and trust. We want to pray for your ship. We want to ask God to bless your ship. We will pray in our way as Muslims. And you pray in your way as followers of Jesus."

And so we did.

After months of work in The Gambia, we received a letter from President A. J. Yahya Jammeh. "We cannot thank you enough," he wrote. "Not only have you treated my people and taken care of them, but you have also taught them valuable lessons, the most important being love and respect." And he also put those beautiful words into action by personally underwriting the costs of two of his countrymen to serve onboard our hospital ship.

The Muslim village elders and their prayer brought home another reality of Africa. To work in Africa is not only to live with the results of history, but also with history in the making—the politics of our time. And that includes the Muslim/Christian tensions that face us in the twenty-first century.

Many people don't think of African nations as being Muslim. But West Africa, sub-Saharan Africa, is a land of Muslim countries. Many are 50 to 90 percent Muslim. Several, such as Guinea, are almost 100 percent Muslim. And Africa hasn't escaped the same inbred tensions between their own Christian and Muslim factions, equally as bloody and explosive as the rest of the world's, and growing alarmingly more so each year. Other countries, far from the Middle East, countries we hope one day to visit with a Mercy Ship, are also Muslim by faith. Indonesia, for instance, is the largest Muslim nation in the world. And that makes the questions concerning our motives even more loaded from a geopolitical point of view.

You can imagine, then, how sensitive and doubly cautious the Mercy Ships crew has to be in a Muslim nation when our motives are questioned. "What do we have to do to be helped by your surgeons?" they ask, waiting for the hook.

"Nothing," we reply, as always. "We do it for free. There is no catch." In a Muslim context, though, the question then takes on another dimension: "Is there a religious creed I have to subscribe to?"

"Absolutely not," we answer, as we always answer. "We will perform the surgery on you or your child without any pre-qualifications whatsoever, and we will send you home."

Then we explain that there has never been any pressure or coercion on an individual as a precondition to receiving our services or help of any kind, and that there never will be. Before we enter any nation, we sign a protocol with top government officials to assuage such fears. We have been invited back to every nation where a Mercy Ship has served, including Muslim nations.

Interestingly enough, I initially declined the very first invitation we received from a Muslim nation. The nation was Guinea, which is almost 100 percent Muslim. The invitation came during our first trip to Togo. I decided not to accept it. And soon I received a visit from a handful of the nation's civic leaders and health authorities who were in Togo for a World Bank meeting.

"What might we say to persuade you to bring your hospital ship to our people?" they asked.

I had a list of reservations, I told them, trying to be as polite as I could.

"Would you mind sharing them?" one of them asked.

"First," I explained. "I don't think we are ready." We had just experienced our very first year in Africa. At the time they visited us, we had eighteen different nationalities in the medical department alone—doctors, dentists, nurses, and lab technicians from Africa, Europe, Australia, New Zealand, the Dominican Republic, and the United States. And while we were learning quickly how to adapt and work with each other's many different cultures and languages, I truly didn't think we were ready to work in a Muslim nation—yet.

"Second," I admitted, "I'm not certain we could get the assurances needed that we won't be the targets of the radical Islamic elements within a Muslim nation." Even then it was a threat worldwide.

On I went, going down my list, one by one. One by one, they countered every concern. Still, I was very hesitant, and told them so.

Then one of them said perhaps the one thing I could not ignore: "Do you know of the hospital ship *Hope*?"

"Yes," I said. "It's one of the models we studied to become what we are."

"Did you know the *Hope* visited here twenty-five years ago?"

That got my attention.

"And did you know," he added, "that our nation's families still talk about the wonderful work the ship did here, to this day?"

As you might imagine, we went to Guinea. In fact, we went the very next year. That encounter taught me a valuable lesson about the common ground of medicine, its incredible power, and the hope it offers as a basis on which mutual trust can grow.

And I also learned that with much of the Muslim world, surprisingly enough, the way to engage their culture with respect often means meeting them on common ground.

Two of my favorite Mercy Ships stories involve Muslim patients, offering hope beyond religion and politics through the mercy of medicine.

The first one begins with the crafting of artificial eyeballs. During our visit to Guinea, a Muslim judge, unable to find help for his little boy, came to our screening day.

"Do I have to become a Christian first? Pray in Jesus' name and follow him?" the judge had asked warily during the screening.

We told him we would operate on his little boy the same as we would anyone else, with no preconditions whatsoever.

"But you are Christian," he said, studying our reactions carefully.

"Most of us are but not all of us," we told him. "What we do is an expression of God's love, much like Mother Teresa has done in Calcutta. The model for our efforts is the model of Jesus. And for Mercy Ships, that includes healing those who are sick, with no strings attached."

He considered that for a moment, and then allowed our team to examine his little boy. Glaucoma was destroying the little boy's eye. When the doctors said they could provide a glass eye, the judge allowed them to take his son onboard. The boy, whose name was Alseny, stayed onboard for ten days, time enough for the surgery, healing, and fitting of the prosthetic eye. His father and older brother came to see him every day.

Prosthetist Paul Moehring, a dental technician from Texas, who joined the crew to make dental bridges and crowns, had quickly become the creative genius behind such custom needs as artificial teeth, ears, eyes, noses, even prosthesis models for jaw replacement operations. We gave him a closet-size office crammed under the bow of the ship, where he stuffed his gizmos, along with a stereo that wafted Mozart down the corridors as he worked.

I was there when he made three prosthetic eyes for Alseny. After he made one to fit Alseny's eight-year-old face, Paul then measured the diameter of his father's and older brother's eyes in order to estimate the size of two larger eyeballs—one to fit Alseny in his early to late teens, and a third one to fit him as an adult.

When little Alseny saw his face in a mirror for the first time with his new artificial eye, his smile was so bright, it almost lit up the entire room. And soon, he was holding the box with the other eyeballs ready for his future face as well.

On the day that the judge, along with his elder son, came to take the boy home, some of the civic and government leaders who had opened the door for us to come to Guinea happened to be onboard visiting us. We were all standing in the reception area when little Alseny, beaming, came rushing into the room and ran to his older brother, who had not yet seen his new eye. The brother twirled him around, both of them laughing excitedly at his new "look."

The judge turned to me in front of the Guinea leaders and said, "This is my youngest boy, and I love him greatly. Other children threw stones at him and called him names, yelling that 'the Great Satan' had entered him. I couldn't find any help nor could I protect him, even though I am a judge in my nation's second largest city. Then I came to you on this hospital ship, and you helped us for free."

He smiled, watching little Alseny show his brother his box of eye-balls. "Muslims are told in the Koran of the Injil—what you call the Gospels—and to honor the People of the Book, all Jews and Christians," he continued. "I have not become a Christian, but because you have helped my son when no one else could, I am reading the Injil to learn more about this loving side of Allah, and . . ." he added, with a wink, "I'm praying in Jesus' name, just in case."

A second story involves another such surprise, with a twist. An ophthalmologist from Texas, a Jewish Christian proud of his heritage, has volunteered on our ships several times. On this trip, his very first patient was a blind African mullah, the religious leader of a mosque. The mullah told the doctor through a translator, "I want you to operate on my eyes so I can once again study the Koran and teach my people how to live."

When the doctor heard this, he excused himself from the operating room to go outside. His internal dialogue went something like this: *I've just taken two long flights to the other side of the world. I miss my wife and kids. I'm losing thousands of dollars in operating revenue in my home practice, and my first patient is a Muslim mullah? Is this really what I should do?*

And after a few tense moments, he had the impression that he should do the best possible surgery he could because God loved the mullah as much as God loved him. So he returned to the operating room. What he didn't know was that the nurses had been talking to the mullah and had mentioned that the doctor was Jewish. Guess who had the problem now?

The mullah, all too aware of what was happening in the Middle East, suddenly wasn't so sure he wanted this Jewish doctor, with his set of surgical knives, working on him.

Here was the geopolitical situation of the world in a microcosm, and it was happening onboard our ship, right before our very eyes. Finally, the mullah consented, and the doctor performed the surgery. All went well.

Before the doctor left to go home, one of our follow-up team returned to the ship, looking for him. "We want you to know what is happening before you leave," the team member explained. The mullah told them that, although he was skilled in knowledge of the Koran, he had never experienced such a loving community. He remembered our explanation of the mercy found on Mercy Ships. Since we were People of the Book and studying our book was part of a good Muslim's duty, he had told the people in his mosque that the only way to discover this loving nature of the character of God would be through studying the Injil. So the mullah procured video equipment and was playing a video version of the gospel of Luke in his mosque to teach them what he learned from a Jewish doctor about a God of love.

Sometimes we find ourselves working with the all-too-recent wounds of war, the kind of history humanity knows all too well. Mercy Ships doctors have performed war-related surgeries after civil wars in such places as Sierra Leone and Nicaragua—maimings from machete attacks, limb losses from land mines, all the things you imagine during war's atrocities. Often, the walking wounded come to us through the country's medical, religious, and humanitarian agencies, sometimes brought by one of these selfless workers personally. The story of Tamba is a marvelous example.

When rebel forces swept through his village, Tamba told us that he remembered hearing gunfire and screaming. He immediately joined a stampede of villagers running for their lives. They all ran for a low bridge between the village and the bush to hide, but the rebels followed. Tamba jumped from the low bridge and took cover. When he felt a prod by a soldier's boot, he knew it was over. He caught the sudden movement of a machete slicing through the air toward his neck. He ducked sideways, and the next thing he knew he was clutching a pulpy mass that had been the right side of his face. He heard the soldiers laughing as they left him to die. "You're good for nothing now, friend," one of the soldiers had sneered.

Somehow Tamba stumbled through the bush until an older couple found him and took him in. The days and weeks blurred as infection set in on what was left of his face. He finally decided to try to return home to die. While there, he met a human rights worker named Eva, who took Tamba to a nongovernmental organization, Médecins Sans Frontieres (Doctors Without Borders), where their medical personnel began to treat him. When they'd done their best, he was still missing a large part of his cheeks, one side of his nose, and most of the flesh covering both his upper and lower jaws.

Tamba returned to his job as an auto mechanic and learned to get through his village by keeping his head down and his face covered. But each glimpse in a mirror pushed him further into depression. One day, Eva told him of a Mercy Ship coming to Freetown. Tamba shrugged. He wasn't interested. He'd lost all hope long ago. Finally, friends from MSF persuaded him to go with them to the ship's screening. There, the doctor he met uttered words he never thought he'd hear: *"I think we can help you."*

Three surgeries would be required, but soon he'd have a face again. After his first surgery, the nurses began to notice that his eyes were twinkling above the bandages. One day, he joked about the day he'd have to shave the mustache that would now grow from the parts of his scalp the doctors had used to rebuild his face. Finally the day came when he was able to look at himself in the mirror and smile once again.

Injuries from traditions may break our hearts most of all, because they are so preventable. We see our share of botched procedures. The African tradition of female genital mutilation known as FGM has attracted worldwide outrage in recent years. Millions of girls are subjected to female genital mutilation every year. The story that tugs at my heart is little Kumbuna. Two and one-half years old, chestnut eyes, tiny braids around her head like a halo, babbling in a Serahule dialect, she was cheerful and healthy except for one thing—a botched female circumcision that made urinating all but impossible for the toddler.

Ignoring the protest of a father who demanded that his daughter remain untouched, Kumbuna's grandmother, a powerful figure in their tribe, insisted the ritual take place. But the tradition was shoddily done, and the razor cuts resulted in scar tissue forming over her urethra. Her mother brought her to a Mercy Ship, where the doctors performed the surgery she needed. The team knew little Kumbuna's healing was going to be incredibly painful. So they kept Kumbuna and her mother in the ship's ward, so she could be given medicine to help her through the awful pain.

"The grandmother is now dead," her mother told the nurses. "If not, I would bring her here so she could see what she has done." Weeks later, both mother and child returned for her final post-operative check. They were both smiling. They were both happy. The scars will always be with Kumbuna, but the pain is gone. And we can only hope that her future will be one that will see an end to this barbaric female ritual.

As we began to see such specific problems facing so many African women, Mercy Ships vowed to bring justice as well as healing to them. In recent years, we've made vesicovaginal fistula (VVF) surgeries one of our specialties. A 2004 BBC Worldwide report highlighted the work of Mercy Ships in battling the problem. The report called it a "female medical crisis the world is only just beginning to understand."

Childbearing in the developing world can be life-threatening, with the mother in as much danger as the child. But the mother—like Akou, whose story opened this chapter—is also in danger of damage done to other organs, including the bladder, that can cause nonstop urine leakage. That leads to embarrassment and ostracism for the vast majority of African women. They face the same potential social problems as those with other serious disfigurements—abandonment by their husbands and families, and sometimes even their children are taken away from them. So Mercy Ships has begun to offer these special surgeries to correct this condition and restore women to wholeness.

Ethiopia's Addis Ababa Fistula Hospital, world renowned for its pioneering work in fistula surgeries, trains and sends surgeons all over the developing world to help organizations like ours. The hospital was founded by Australian Drs. Catherine and Reg Hamlin in 1975 and has successfully operated on more than twenty thousand women.

Following her husband's death, Catherine continued the work and ultimately was nominated for the 1999 Nobel Peace Prize, immortalizing their story in the book *The Hospital by the River*. Two of their specialists came to offer their services during our Sierra Leone visit in 2003: the current director, Dr. Andrew Browning, and a special woman named Mamitu Gafhi, who has performed more than two thousand surgeries and whose own story is remarkable.

As a young Ethiopian bride, Gafhi endured six days of excruciating labor. Her baby was stillborn, and complications left her with VVF. After a series of surgeries and more complications, she was told the hard truth— her condition was too extreme for correction. She would never be healed. Mamitu turned the tables and dedicated her life to helping other women with VVF who could be healed. She stayed on at the Ethiopian hospital, learning to perform VVF procedures on her own. Along with both Drs. Hamlin, Mamitu Gafhi was cited on the Gold Medal for Surgery from the Royal College of Surgeons in London. Forty years later, she is still performing the surgery. Only four doctors worldwide have performed more VVF surgeries than this one African woman who decided not to give up and dedicated her life to giving back.

Every woman, after VVF surgery onboard a Mercy Ship, is given a new dress as a symbol of her brighter future. And quite often, a group of these women will burst into joyous dance and song after their recovery, dancing down our gangways into normal life. It is a sight to behold. And you can imagine how the crew loves joining each and every celebration.

To interact with Africa is to work with the past and the present, in all its forms and challenges. With the weight of history and politics always near, these amazing years in Africa have taught us so much. We aim to act as healing agents in every possible way; we meet nations where they want to be met, through dialogue and relationship building, focusing on what we have in common.

In this way, sailing with mutual respect and care, Mercy Ships should continue to enjoy the humbling privilege of offering hope and healing in every port of call. And when I doubt this is true, I hear the Guinea Muslim leaders: "Did you know our families still talk about the time the hospital ship *Hope* visited here twenty-five years ago?"

My hope is that years from now the same will be said for the hospital fleet called Mercy Ships, that they become a part of history too—a tool of reconciliation for all.

FROM THE BRIDGE

Excerpted from *Mercy Ships News,*
all editions, March 2000

Bulletin:
Latest News of Mercy Ships Fleet

Caribbean Mercy

The ship's cargo holds were full as she left in February for her return medical port call to El Salvador. Telemundo, a Latin television station, has agreed to cover the president and first lady's visit to the ship . . .

Anastasis

While sailing from Cape Town to The Gambia, the crew sterilized the O.R. suite. On February 1, following two successful surgical screening days during which 386 patients received appointments, surgeries got under way.

In the town of Brikama, about an hour's drive from Banjul's harbor, the dental team established their dental clinic. On Feb. 3–4 the village medical team began their daily clinics in the Kombo Central District at Kassa Kunda, an area which does not have easy access to medical facilities . . .

New Ship (soon to be *Africa Mercy*)

Architectural plans have been drawn up to convert the ship to a hospital vessel, and work on the vessel continues at a steady pace. The new crew is setting up operations onboard.

The naming ceremony for the new ship has been set for April 4th. People from all over the world are flying to Newcastle for this milestone event . . .

SHIP'S LOG:
1990–2005

● ● ●

Longitude/Latitude: The World

CHAPTER 10

TO THE ENDS OF THE EARTH

If there are poor on the moon, we will go there too.

—Mother Teresa

It takes nearly 30,000 miles to circumnavigate the globe by ocean. By the turn of the century, the *Anastasis* had sailed 182,831 miles. The combined miles of all Mercy Ships as we sailed into the twenty-first century was easily the equivalent of a dozen trips around the world . . . and counting.

After that pivotal winter of 1991, we found a routine, sailing along the West African coast and back again to Europe. Except for one year when the ship returned to the United States, and another, when it went to South Africa, the *Anastasis* plied that same route, spending four to seven months at one or two countries a year before sailing back to Europe for maintenance, recruiting, and fund-raising. Each year, our screenings became larger, the medical volunteers busier, the recovery wards fuller, and the partnering opportunities on land more plentiful. The next year, in 1992, our two ports of call were the Ivory Coast and Guinea.

The third year, Sierra Leone was our only port, but not actually by choice. You can't live and work on a ship and not have your share of nautical misadventures. That year, while in Sierra Leone, the ship's boiler broke down. Taking a positive approach, the crew made the most of it by extending the field service to that country until a brand-new boiler could be installed. After that, we sailed to the U.S. for the required maintenance, recruiting, and fund-raising routine. Then in 1994–95 we returned to Africa for a long visit to Ghana.

In 1996, after a return visit to Togo, we sailed due south. Apartheid had just been abolished. So in the same spirit as our visit to Poland in 1990, we sailed to South Africa to support that amazing freedom event. The South Africa visit was the only time in which the *Anastasis* could "do it all" in one country—dry dock maintenance, recruitment, and fund-raising, as well as medical and dental treatments. That allowed us to spend over an entire year on the continent of Africa. Ahead were visits to Benin, Guinea, The Gambia, and Senegal. Then came the long-awaited return to Sierra Leone.

When Mercy Ships first visited Sierra Leone in 1992–93, some of the patients who underwent surgeries needed follow-up operations. So we had promised to return in the next year or so. We gave these patients "return appointment cards" for the follow-up care. Little did we know that we would not be able to return to Sierra Leone for a decade. Civil war erupted almost immediately after we left the country. When we did return in 2001, the crew didn't know who would, or even could, return after the long rebel war.

When I think of that return visit, and the anticipation the crew felt waiting to see if any of their former patients would arrive, I think of Patrick Coker. Before his surgery, Patrick lived with a jaw tumor that had been growing since he was eight years old. *(see photos 7 and 8)* In 1993, Chief Medical Officer Dr. Gary Parker performed two operations on Patrick, removing the tumor and affected portions of his lower jaw and inserting a titanium implant. Patrick spent two weeks in the recovery ward as he healed. His next surgery would replace the titanium plate with one of his own bones. When the ship sailed, Patrick had his return card in hand for that follow-up operation.

Then the civil war began. During those years, Patrick married and had three children. Anticipating the horrific rebel attack on Freetown that happened in 1999, he sent his family to another village. When the rebels stormed the city, Patrick became trapped at his father-in-law's house, along with 150 others.

Yelling threats of death and maiming, the rebel force began burning houses, forcing out those in hiding. Patrick could hear the screams of the ones caught, knowing the rebels were cutting off their hands. As they came closer and closer to the house where Patrick and the others hid, a woman on the street began to put up a loud ruckus. The rebels, distracted, moved on, missing the house and all those in it, sparing Patrick and all with him.

That was the story Patrick told us when he arrived in 2002 for his long-awaited follow-up surgery. The very next year, when we returned, he underwent his fourth and final operation, his transformation finally fully complete.

Sierra Leone itself, however, was another thing. Already classified as the poorest nation of the world, the country was literally in shambles, decimated by war. The vision of Mercy Ships had always been to go where we were most needed. So, in the years ahead, we made a commitment to Sierra Leone. It would become a place we returned to again and again, and then, after the turn of the century, a place where we chose to have a full-time presence.

Meanwhile, the other side of the globe was not without its Mercy Ships drama as well. All through the late 1980s and early 1990s, the *Good Samaritan* had been serving the Caribbean in relief and medical outreach efforts. She had even made one trip to the South Pacific and one to the edge of the African continent, as well as two trips to South America. Her crew took her up the Amazon River, taking dentists into villages far inland. The "Little Giant" also had a brush with worldwide athletic fame. The U.S. Olympic Committee paid to renovate the ship, enabling her for service to the Pan American Games in Havana, Cuba. The *Good Samaritan* was the first vessel in thirty years to sail from America to communist Cuba with U.S. governmental permission.

But the "Little Giant" just wasn't big enough for the dream we had of a floating eye-surgery hospital for the Caribbean and Central America. So in 1994 we bought a Norwegian coastal cruise ship, renamed it the *Caribbean Mercy,* and began transforming it into the floating eye hospital of our Mercy Ships dreams. The "*Good Sam*" was just the right size for ports in the South Pacific. We renamed the ship the *Island Mercy* and moved it into service there to join the *Pacific Ruby,* a small, donated yacht used for relief work in the South Pacific area for a short time during the early 1990s.

The *Island Mercy* was right at home in the South Pacific. In 1999, for instance, the crew treated more than twenty-four thousand patients in six nations from Tonga to the Philippines, partnering with local groups in new and wonderful ways.

In Gilligan City, Philippines, for example, the local Kiwanis Club had prescreened a group of the region's neediest people for dental and optical assessments, and local dentists and opticians had joined the *Island Mercy* crew to help meet the demand. While in Manila, during the same Philippine visit, the ship's crew also saw 135 Filipinos a day during a medical field service with people who lived in the city's garbage dumps. This type of service would become the norm for the little Mercy Ship.

Meanwhile, the *Caribbean Mercy*, Mercy Ship's newest fleet member, performed its initial act of mercy before it even docked at its first port. On the way to her first medical assignment in the Dominican Republic, with a new crew of eighty-one, including several families, the *Caribbean Mercy* sailed not only into bad weather and high seas, but also into the path of history.

About eight miles off the northeast coastline of Cuba, in whitecap waves, one of the crew sighted a small boat in distress. The people in the boat were frantically waving for help. Their boat was taking on water. The captain of the *Caribbean Mercy* immediately radioed the U.S. Coast Guard, asking for permission to help. When the Coast Guard gave the okay, the Mercy Ship moved as close to the boat as possible and pulled the people onboard just before it sank.

Over the next twenty-four hours, as the *Caribbean Mercy* continued slowly eastward against buffeting winds, the crew cared for the twenty-four people who explained they were Cuban refugees trying to escape to the United States. The next afternoon, a Coast Guard vessel arrived and took the refugees into their charge.

This wouldn't be the last time the *Caribbean Mercy* would find itself drawn into the drama of historical events. Just a few months later, the Mercy Ship partnered with a humanitarian group to carry a cargo of high-protein food made especially for the needs of malnourished people in Haiti. On Christmas Eve 1994, we made a short stop at the port of Gonaives, Haiti, to deliver the food, supplies, and aid to a local orphanage and hospital.

United States military troops were stationed in Haiti on a peacekeeping mission at that time, following a political revolt. The entire country was in a state of civil war and economic chaos that resulted in the infamous Haiti "boat people" refugee crisis. United States Army paratroopers from Fort Bragg, North Carolina, were stationed in Gonaives, and several of the soldiers patrolled the dock area where the *Caribbean Mercy* was located. On Christmas Day, eight of the soldiers came onboard to enjoy an evening dinner and special Christmas program with the crew. One of the soldiers was Army Sergeant Greg Cardott, who seemed to especially connect with the crew, a mutual bonding that he mentioned in letters to his wife.

Just two weeks after the ship left Haiti, Sergeant Cardott was killed while manning a highway checkpoint near Gonaives, the only American soldier to die in the entire peacekeeping mission. Nine months later, the crew of the *Caribbean Mercy,* knowing the ship would be docked at a port for a short time near Fort Bragg, invited his widow and two daughters to spend a weekend onboard. In October 1995, Greg's widow, a registered nurse, along with his daughters, spent time onboard while the ship was docked at Morehead City, North Carolina. The crew wanted to get to know her, and she wanted to know them.

The *Caribbean Mercy* soon began following the same yearly pattern as her big sister, the *Anastasis.* The ship would spend several months in the United States for maintenance and fund-raising in order to spend the rest of the year in the Caribbean basin and Central America. Each year the ship served the Caribbean's neediest residents, in nations that partnered with us, such as the Dominican Republic, Nicaragua, El Salvador, Guatemala, Honduras, and Haiti, establishing local friendships and professional relationships with government agencies and medical, charitable, humanitarian, and religious organizations on land.

What was a typical *Caribbean Mercy* port call like? A good example might be one of our visits to El Salvador. If you could have a bird's-eye view of the ship, you'd see short-term volunteer crew heading down the gangway into the city and countryside. Orthopedic surgeons would be headed to the hospital in La Union, optometrists to the nearby army base, and Health Care Teams ferried to the nearby islands by the navy. The Health Care Teams would include audiologists fitting hearing aids, well-drillers searching for water, and dentists looking for cavities. Back onboard, you would see ophthalmologists preparing to operate, and maybe you'd catch a glimpse of the President and First Lady of El Salvador visiting the ship.

Through the years, we have had many distinguished persons visit our floating eye hospital. The First Lady of the Republic of Honduras, Doña Mary Flake de Flores, visited the *Caribbean Mercy* three times during one port call. I recall her participation in one of those special moments when the bandages come off and a blind person suddenly sees—the kind I'd first experienced in Lazaros Cardenas. During her visit to the recovery room, the First Lady had asked one of the patients if she might be the one to remove the patient's eye patch. He had enthusiastically agreed. Slowly she had peeled away the patch, and the face of the First Lady of his country was the first image the patient saw.

In 2004, the new First Lady of the Republic of Honduras, Doña Aguas Ocaña de Maduro, who played a major role in the *Caribbean Mercy* return visit to Honduras, flew in by helicopter for a special reception. When she left, she took along a little girl and her mother in the helicopter to seek specialized medical treatment for the girl's facial tumor.

An amazing *Caribbean Mercy* success story is that of Isabelle. In 1999, as part of the medical outreach team that regularly goes into a port city's hospitals for screenings and subsequent surgeries, orthopedic surgeon and Mercy Ships career crew member Dr. Tim Browne met little Isabelle. Ten-year-old Isabelle had been brought to the El Salvador screening from a little village two hours away, because of her feet. Born with both feet turned completely backward, she had never been able to walk or wear shoes. To get around, Isabelle dragged herself on the tops of her feet. Working together with local surgeons, after several surgeries, Dr. Browne eventually managed to turn Isabelle's feet in the normal direction.

As you might imagine, the "before and after" pictures show an astounding change. But for Isabelle, wearing shoes was the most astounding change. When the Mercy Ship was back in El Salvador the very next year, a team paid a follow-up visit to see how Isabelle was doing. The team traveled to her little village and found Isabelle doing well. They discovered, though, that she had a baby sister who was just learning to walk on club feet. The team made arrangements for Isabelle's little sister to be operated on as well.

In 2001, while the ship was docked in Guatemala, the *Caribbean Mercy* experienced an earthquake to rival the *Anastasis'* experience in Greece. Working in a tropical weather zone, never knowing what might happen next, the crew usually keeps the ship's holds as full of emergency supplies as possible. So when the ground suddenly shook, and the sea began to rock and roll under the ship, the ship was ready to help.

The crew learned that the epicenter was in neighboring El Salvador. Hundreds were killed, and hundreds of thousands were left homeless. A medical team from the ship sprang into action. Assembling supplies on hand, the crew returned to El Salvador to join the relief efforts, where aftershocks continued while they helped the injured and homeless.

Part of our crew's routine involved working at health clinics on-shore, and where there was no clinic, sometimes pitching in with the locals and building one. Homes, churches, clinics, wells, orphanages, latrines—Mercy Ships short-term volunteer crew, bringing their expertise along with them, have built them all. With such talent, we began setting up land-based resource and support offices around the world, including a land base in Nicaragua and in Sierra Leone.

With each passing year, the world began to feel smaller. We began to dream of filling the oceans with a fleet of seagoing ships of mercy. We began to think big, not just in possibilities, but also in size. For the work we were doing, we decided that all future Mercy Ships should be as big as the *Anastasis*. We needed more operating rooms to allow for more operations at each port stay, more recovery rooms, more rooms for the crew—more room for more of everything.

So by the turn of the century, we made plans to say good-bye to the *Island Mercy* and *Pacific Ruby* and throw all our resources into acquiring ships big enough to take in our growing vision. We began to brainstorm plans for this new growing fleet idea—an *Africa Mercy*, an *Asia Mercy*, and an *Atlantic Mercy*. And as we were just beginning to envision such ships, out of the blue we received an invitation from the North Korean embassy representative in Switzerland to bring the *Caribbean Mercy* to their country.

Historically we knew the development of new contacts for Mercy Ships was linked to a visit of a ship, so we accepted, seeing this perhaps as a first step toward an Asian Mercy Ship. We made plans to specialize in eye surgeries, train some of the North Korean eye surgeons in new techniques, provide a million dollars' worth of new surgical equipment, and bring rice and relief materials. The protocol was signed, and soon we were en route.

We brought the *Caribbean Mercy* through the Panama Canal up the Pacific coast of Central America, toward Alaska. From Seattle we sailed on the inside passage to Seward, Kodiak Island, with short stops in Petropavlovsk, Russia. *(see photo 9)* We sailed through ten time zones and seven bodies of water, and just as we were within one hundred miles of North Korea, we were notified that the conditions of our invitation were rescinded. Only days before, vessels from North and South Korea had engaged in an incident over territorial fishing water rights. North and South Korea navies exchanged fire, and thirty North Koreans were killed.

The North Korean government, although they had previously agreed to waive all port charges and welcome us, now told us they had changed their minds. They now wanted to charge us ten thousand dollars a day port fees with no guarantee as to when the ship would be offloaded or how long we would have to stay. Immediately we could see a scenario where this could become a financial nightmare, or worse. We feared that the ship, albeit on a mission of charity, might become a hostage in the middle of this dispute.

So we made the decision not to continue the voyage to North Korea. Sadly, we sailed instead for Dalian, China, where we offloaded our supplies and transferred them to a partner charity that would send the goods to help the people of Vietnam.

However, one moment in our visit to Dalian reminded me again of the need for an *Asia Mercy* ship. I met with the Chinese delegate to the World Health Organization during that time. We were discussing the *Caribbean Mercy*'s eye-surgery expertise when I mentioned the often-quoted World Health Organization's statistic of sixty million needy blind in the world. I'll never forget her response:

"We have done the best we can to get statistics, but we all realize we could have sixty million blind in China alone. There is ample opportunity for us to partner with you and your ship right here."

Later when the December 26, 2004, tsunami struck Asia, killing hundreds of thousands, we again sensed the need for a Mercy Ship in Asia in an even deeper way.

And so we continue to dream.

After three months in South Korea, laying the groundwork for a future Mercy Ship for Asia, the *Caribbean Mercy* took the opportunity to sail into the Philippines for a historic meeting with the *Island Mercy* and a medical-assignment partnership in Pulupandan, Philippines, before sailing back via Manila to its Caribbean basin home. A local marching band in brightly colored uniforms greeted us—a marvelous sight after the North Korean experience, to say the least.

When we came close, the *Island Mercy* blew her horn and sent up five flares, much to our delight. We learned that to enable the bigger *Caribbean Mercy* to come into port, the island's dredger had to work overtime to make the channel deep enough, and had broken down twice in as many days. But soon the two sister ships were berthed side by side, performing eye surgeries on the *Caribbean Mercy* and running a dental clinic onboard the *Island Mercy.*

By the turn of a new century, Mercy Ships had grown into a thirty-four-million-dollar-per-year nonprofit hospital ship charity, with offices in sixteen nations, a growing fleet, and an international board reflecting the diverse background and expertise of our crew. We had become Mercy Ships International. We all knew it was finally time for the next ship—something bigger, newer, state-of-the-art, a ship to take us into the next chapter of Mercy Ships, to begin planning the fleet of our dreams.

But what happened next surprised us all.

ANGEL OF MERCY

PR Newswire Association, Inc., 2002

Headline: Ann Gloag: Angel of Mercy
Dateline: London, Edinburgh, Glasgow, Los Angeles

Ann Gloag is a volunteer on a one-of-a-kind floating hospital Mercy Ship on which she is a volunteer with a mop and a broom. There are other volunteers with similar chores. So what is so unusual about Ms. Gloag doing these necessary menial chores? She is the richest woman in Scotland, one of the wealthiest in the U.K. and founder of the multi-million pound Stagecoach Empire.

Ms. Gloag, a former nurse, has become a guardian angel of Mercy, donating 4 million pounds, the biggest donation Mercy Ships has received in its history, to help build a Mercy Ship.

The Africa Mercy *is the first addition in a proposed new plan to add ships to the existing fleet of floating hospitals that visit more than 70 ports worldwide, providing free medical and surgical procedures that bring health, hope, and training to people who would never be able to afford such services . . .*

SHIP'S LOG:
2000–2004

● ● ●

Newcastle, England
55°02' N, 01°42' W

CHAPTER 11

HEADLINES TELL THE STORY

The quality of mercy it is twice blessed: It blesseth him that gives and him that takes.

—*"Merchant of Venice"*, William Shakespeare

"Dame Norma Major to Christen New Mercy Ship!" read the headline.

From around the world, we traveled to the Newcastle shipyard on the River Tyne to stand at the edge of a dock. The Naming Ceremony of the *Africa Mercy*, the newest member of the Mercy Ships fleet, had just begun.

"I am delighted to be standing here with you as we celebrate the many voyages of hope and healing that lie ahead. It now gives me great pleasure to name this ship the *Africa Mercy*. May God bless her, and all who sail on her," said Dame Norma Major, wife of former British Prime Minister John Major. Then she shot a champagne bottle from a launcher, the bottle smashed against the side of the ship, and the master of ceremonies of the shipyard led the crowd in three cheers as a bagpipe band began to play.

Why the bagpipes? In honor of Ann Gloag, the Scottish woman who had made the day possible.

This day was a wonderful surprise to us all. Our strategic planning, our vision for the future, called for a new fleet of Mercy Ships—one for every continent. Only recently had we decided the time was right for the first new ship. Our flagship, the *Anastasis*, was more than fifty years old. The ship was extremely well built. But even if it stayed afloat forever, the need in Africa was so great that we knew an *Africa Mercy* was the next logical addition to our fleet. We also knew buying a big ship was going to be much more expensive this time around, so we began meeting people and courting corporations, hoping to build up a healthy bank balance toward the purchase.

Then in 1998, we met a woman who had already researched us, having come to the same conclusions as we had about the value of floating hospitals. We also discovered that she had investigated us with the same attention to detail that had made her one of the U.K.'s most successful businesswomen. For Mercy Ships that was a very good thing. She pored over our annual audit and met administrators, surgeons, and board members. Finally, she found we embodied "precisely the qualities necessary for running a successful business, the sheer efficiency of the operation, and the low cost of the delivery of the service," as she put it.

Gloag, trained in nursing, first became interested in Africa when her company began operating bus services in Malawi and Kenya. During her early years as a nurse, she'd worked in a burns unit and was shocked to discover that African children with untreated superficial burns were dying from infections. So for several years, she supplied and supported a burns unit at a hospital in the country, even after the Stagecoach Bus Company ceased operations there.

As she told the *London Telegraph* magazine in 2001, that experience had made her acutely aware of the problems inherent in providing health care in developing nations. Surgeons she brought to the hospital were not able to operate because surgical instruments were missing or stolen, or because the electricity or water wasn't working. "But a ship that sailed in fully equipped and which is effective from the day that it docks just struck me as the way forward."

I'll never forget the moment she told us what she'd already decided. I had just met her. In August 1998, the *Anastasis* was docked at London, and I'd invited her onboard for a tour. At the end of it, Ann turned to me and said, "I'll buy your next ship." I couldn't believe I'd heard what I thought I'd heard. She must have seen the look on my face, because she repeated it:

"I'll buy your next ship."

I was speechless.

Since then, Ann has joined her world-class enthusiasm and worldwide contacts with us, to raise the fifty-two million dollars necessary to purchase, renovate, and equip the next ship. She has also joined the executive committee of the International Board, becoming actively involved in fund-raising, budgets, and strategic planning.

In short order, we found a Danish ferry that had the space and the promise of a hospital ship of our dreams. We bought it, moved it to the British shipyard, and began the fund-raising needed to transform the huge ship into the *Africa Mercy*, scheduled to sail by 2005.

In 2002, when Mercy Ships leaders were invited to the inauguration of Benin's President Mathieu Kérékou, Ann traveled with us and stayed for two weeks, serving on the ship in the hospital ward. She also found herself stuck in the mud with the rest of us, on our way to visit a village health clinic, pushing our four-wheel vehicles out of the mud during a downpour. She told us she loved every minute.

During the past few years, the transformation of Mercy Ships into a global charity has inspired many headlines, but even the quieter events were headline material to us. Hundreds of wonderful daily news events added up to big news for us at Mercy Ships International.

A sampling of those headlines tells the story of this new chapter as we sail into the future:

Great Scot! It's Mercy Ships!!

"Volunteers Receive Charity Award in Home Nation of Scotland," read the headline. Mercy Ships seems to have been blessed with great Scots at pivotal moments in our transformation. And we weren't the only ones who noticed. Scotland's leading newspaper, Glasgow's *Sunday Mail,* honored Ann Gloag and Lord Ian McColl as recipients of their nation's 2002

Great Scot Award for their charity involvement on behalf of Mercy Ships. Readers nominate unsung heroes for the award that has become nationally known as "Scotland's People's Oscar."

> *Scotland's richest businesswoman, Ann Gloag, donated 4 million pounds to purchase a Mercy Ship for the global charity of Mercy Ships and is a passionate supporter of the cause. Professor The Lord McColl, top surgeon at Guy's Hospital in London, is the charity's U.K. spokesman and Vice Chairman of the International Board of Mercy Ships. Both Gloag and McColl currently donate significant amounts of their time and energies toward raising awareness and funding for the completion of the newest vessel in the growing Mercy Ships fleet, the* Africa Mercy. *Both Scots describe Mercy Ships as "good value."*

These two great Scots are symbolic of the many special people, within our truly international scope, who have come onboard with Mercy Ships and are reshaping it with cyclone force—and making headlines as they do.

Mercy Ships to Partner with World's Leading Teaching Hospitals

In March of 2004, Lord McColl was invited to do grand rounds at Harvard Medical School and Brigham and Women's Hospital. Lord McColl, besides being chairman of the board of the U.K. Mercy Ships and vice-chairman of Mercy Ships International, has been the physician to heads of state. While at Harvard, he presented a PowerPoint presentation of some of the surgeries that we do on Mercy Ships. Afterward, one of the hospital's top medical educators asked an unexpected question: "Might our residents spend some time with you on your ships? The pathology that they could be exposed to would take a lifetime to replicate here in the West."

It was true. Lord McColl's colleagues at the teaching hospital saw something we could not. We could teach as well as heal. The developed world had totally eradicated many of the diseases and medical problems we were seeing.

At almost the same time, the University of San Francisco Children's Hospital approached us with similar questions, as did someone from a UK hospital. Would we at Mercy Ships find a way for their residents to come serve with us?

Can you imagine how I felt when I heard this news? Talk about a win/win situation. My hope and prayer is that this may somehow become a reality at some future point.

Mercy Ships Announces Satellite Communications for Fleet

Communications is always a challenge on a ship. Now, though, it's rarely a problem at all for our growing fleet. Between state-of-the-art systems offered us at cost from two leading maritime communications companies, MTN and Petrocom, we now have full-time satellite communication capabilities both in port and at sea.

But there are more reasons to be excited about this news than just ship-to-shore calls. Not only does this give us the twenty-four hour connection to the outside world we have long needed, but it also opens up a whole new dimension to the quality of care we offer in the operating rooms. Now, when surgeons onboard encounter a case they have never seen and they need to know its pathology, we consult by satellite. With a digital camera and new communications technology, we can snap an image; e-mail it to, say, Harvard Medical School for a specialist's opinion on problematic cases; and, in a matter of hours, our surgeons can be given world-class consultation on how to treat their patients. The satellites allow a twenty-first-century synergy like nothing else we've ever experienced, offering a level of medical care and expertise to rival any on the globe.

Matching Grant of $10 Million Given by Anonymous Foundation

In 2002, we received a challenge we excitedly accepted to make the transformation of the *Africa Mercy* happen—a ten-million-dollar grant that would be ours if we were able to match it by raising another ten million dollars. This was a blast of great news for us, and it was an even bigger and better blast when we matched it by 2004. And headlines like the following helped it happen:

Mercy Ships Reception Held at House of Lords
and
Former Prime Minister to Hold News Conference for Global Charity

Prominent British leaders in medicine and politics have magnanimously offered their time to further the cause of Mercy Ships International in both the U.K. and the U.S. Two such moments happened within a year of each other. In September 2002, Lord McColl hosted a reception at the House of Lords. Approximately 135 guests attended the event. The guests learned more about the work of Mercy Ships from Lord McColl, the current chairman of the U.K. board of trustees, and other Mercy Ships leaders. And in April 2003, former British Prime Minister John Major returned to our Texas headquarters as the guest of Mercy Ships. The prime minister spoke on behalf of Mercy Ships in the Dallas–Fort Worth area.

Crew Brings Relief to Abandoned Ship

In February 2004, a Mercy Ship once again came to the rescue of people stranded at sea. As the crew of the *Anastasis* screened patients, scheduled surgeries, and set up programs in Sierra Leone, rumors of an offshore fugitive ship with an abandoned crew and a dead captain piqued their curiosity.

After hearing talk of serious malaria cases onboard the purported fugitive ship, the *Panciu*, the captain of the *Anastasis* found out via web research that the ship had changed names several times. The ship had been detained at least once in ports of call, which seemed to point to "nefarious activity," as the captain put it. And now the crew seemingly had been abandoned so far out to sea that they couldn't help themselves.

The Mercy Ships captain gained permission from the port to do a "humanitarian visit," and he, along with a small contingent of crew, crossed the waters on the ship's launch carrying a few medicines and some food. They found no malaria, but the crew—all from India, Pakistan, or

Bangladesh—were almost out of food and fresh water. They also hadn't been paid for eighteen months and had little prospect of returning to their home countries.

During the next few weeks, when there was time, *Anastasis* deckhands took trips out to the ship to check on the crew. The Mercy Ships captain wrote a letter to the port authorities, helping the abandoned crew get in touch with the International Trade Workers Federation. Weeks later, the crew gratefully received pay and tickets home.

Jebbeh Now Is Saved!

CT Scan Donated Through Volunteer's Benefit Concerts

All our medical moments feel like headlines to us. The two headlines above appeared in print and are perfect examples of the impact one Mercy Ships surgical volunteer can have.

As the number of international medical experts volunteering for Mercy Ships assignments has grown, the ways that word of their work has spread back to their countries and turned into action flowing back to us has been a phenomenal thing to watch.

When maxillofacial surgeon Dr. Luer Köper could not arrange for four-year-old Jebbeh to undergo surgery in Germany, he brought the surgeons to her in Sierra Leone. Dr. Köper first examined Jebbeh in December 2002. The girl was born with an encephalocele, caused by a hole in the skull bones. Children born with this problem die young when meningitis inevitably sets in. Jebbeh was scheduled for a free surgery onboard the Mercy Ship, but her appointment had to be postponed for lack of time.

"I promised her we would come again, and she would have a surgery onboard the ship," Dr. Köper said. Meanwhile, he e-mailed the charity branch of AWD, a Germany economic company that offered funds to take a team of surgeons to Jebbeh. The story of Dr. Köper and Jebbeh was featured in the German newspaper *Bild Am Sonntag*. A retired German journalist saw the coverage and offered to raise funds through a photography exhibition for the remaining cost of Jebbeh's operation. Finally, more than a year after Jebbeh first visited the Mercy Ship, she underwent a successful seven-hour onboard operation. Days later, a German newspaper ran the story with the headline, "Jebbeh Now Is Saved!"

Dr. Köper also noticed that the *Anastasis* was performing its medical miracles without the aid of its own CT scanner. Patients had to be sent to hospitals on land, sometimes into the next country, when surgeons needed a scanner to help in their diagnostic decisions. Even then, the scanners didn't always function properly. So, back home, Dr. Köper organized two benefit concerts for the purchase of a refurbished scanner, and in July 2002, it arrived onboard. We put it to use immediately.

Mercy Ships Doctor Performs Revolutionary Eye Surgery Onboard

In April 2003, onboard the *Caribbean Mercy,* docked at the Dominican Republic, Dr. Glenn Strauss—associate of Heaton Eye Clinic and new director of health care for Mercy Ships, and a pioneer in a new type of eye surgery—performed a procedure known as conductive keratoplasty for the first time ever in a developing nation. The revolutionary painless and quick procedure was performed in selected U.S. sites. For the first time, this world-class treatment was also offered to the poor in the Dominican Republic.

With our emphasis on eye surgery in the Americas and the Caribbean, this operation was a perfect example of the deepening medical partnerships we are creating with top medical consultants all over the world. As Dr. Strauss put it, the procedure was a tremendous Caribbean basin opportunity to "meet the practical vision needs of people who can't get glasses."

Corporate Partners Invigorate Mercy Ships Prowess!

Johnson & Johnson Gives Orthopaedic Supplies Worth Millions

Ophthalmic Laser Technology Provided to Serve Poor

Heaton Eye Associates to Donate Anaesthesia Machine

Kimberly-Clark Lends a Hand to Mercy Ships

Alcon Employees Give Day Off to Create Mercy Ships Packets

One of the biggest reasons for our success as a hospital-ship charity has been our partnership with the corporations who manufacture the medical equipment and materials that make modern medicine so successful. I am a firm believer in the synergy between the corporate world and the charitable. The two need each other. The ways that companies, made up of people like you and me, have begun to partner with us is definitely headline material.

Johnson & Johnson, for instance, has selected Mercy Ships as one of their charities of choice. It has been one of our most successful relationships. In one year alone, they donated $3 million worth of orthopedic supplies. Hundreds of other generous corporations have made our growing errands of medical mercy around the globe not only possible, but economically feasible.

Donations are essential, but sometimes the people who make the products jump in to partner in unique and creative ways. One such story concerns the workers of Alcon, the world's leading eye care company and a major donor of surgical and pharmaceutical ophthalmic products to Mercy Ships, almost from the beginning. When a Mercy Ship docked near Alcon's Houston facility, Vice President and General Manager Sally Wilson took the opportunity to tour the ship. What she saw gave her an idea.

Normally, crew members have to open many donated packets for the exact supplies needed for the Mercy Ship's most commonly performed eye surgery. Wilson thought of a way, with the help of Alcon employees, that the ship's surgeons could use their donations more efficiently. Soon, Alcon employees were enthusiastically volunteering their time to assemble the essential products into a CustomPak Kit designed specifically for Mercy Ships special use. Now when Mercy Ships surgeons operate, they open one packet that contains everything they need. The time saved by this inspired idea allows Mercy Ships surgeons to do more eye surgeries in the time available.

Charity Navigator Gives Mercy Ships Its Highest Rating—Four Stars

In 2002, we were surprised to receive a notice that we had been rated by *Charity Navigator,* a charity comparison website. *Charity Navigator* is an independent charity evaluator, heralded and recognized by publications and entities as diverse as *Reader's Digest,* CNN, the *New York Times, Christian Science Monitor,* and the *Washington Post.* The news was good: Mercy Ships placed in *Charity Navigator*'s highest category for efficiency and vision. They described us as blurring the lines between "previously discrete domains of profits and philanthropy, business and social concerns." Value-based living that "integrates personal and professional concerns is the key to future impact," it went on to say. The summary added:

> *Mercy Ships begins as the story of hardy visionaries retooling an ocean liner to bring medical help to the neediest locales around the world. That essential passion is unchanged. Men and women actually pay for the privilege of living in cramped quarters on a floating city with other volunteers from scores of nations. Some use accumulated wealth, others raise support as charitable staff. All participants, from swabbies to surgeons, have a sense of purpose and job satisfaction that Franklin-Covey (in a recent professional review) rates as among the highest ever encountered.*

(Source: www.charitynavigator.org)

That description of the evolution of our first quarter century captures the spirit of Mercy Ships remarkably well—what we have been, what we want to be, and what we are and always will be.

Mercy Ships Vision Awards Gala Held in Washington, D.C.

In 2002, Mercy Ships hosted a Vision Awards Gala in Washington, D.C., one of the many special opportunities we have had to spend time with leaders of both the developed and developing world who've embraced Mercy Ships' unique charitable vision. That night, we honored the humanitarian efforts of people such as the former first lady of the Republic of Honduras, Mary Flake de Flores; Anthony Hall, U.S. ambassador to the World Food Program in Rome; Daniel Snyder, owner of the NFL Washington Redskins, whose philanthropic organization has gathered more than forty local area businesses to benefit causes such as handicapped children's efforts, literacy, educational, and sports programs; and CNN talk show host Larry King, whose personal foundation, The Larry King Cardiac Foundation helps people who cannot afford to pay for heart disease treatment—including children from Benin, West Africa.

Paying special tribute to such visionaries was memorable. But I also recall the night for its unique sense of perspective. To sit at a Four Seasons

Hotel with influential people in the United States capital city immediately after a months-long Mercy Ship assignment in the world's poorest nation was an odd sensation. And yet it's one I've experienced many times, because such a scenario makes perfect sense from a Mercy Ships point of view. The capacity and desire for mercy in those of us most blessed is the same as that of the people who most need it. And Mercy Ships International's unique and special mission is to be a floating bridge between the two worlds.

And that vision, now in the shape of the 16,071-ton new *Africa Mercy*, doubling the medical mercy we can offer the African continent, inspires us to keep dreaming for the day when there will be a Mercy Ship for every continent, and we will have the privilege of filling the oceans with mercy.

Mercy Ships Begins to Dream of Reaching One Million People a Year

A million people a year served by Mercy Ships—that's our goal. For Mercy Ships International, truly the best is yet to come as we bring hope and healing to the ends of the earth and back again. With the help of just such newsworthy partnerships as these, we hope to be making a million headlines in a million personal lives as we continue to keep sailing, and as we begin to also find our way down the gangway and onto land.

THE STORY OF AMINATA
AND SANDY

Dateline: Freetown, Sierra Leone
8°30' N, 13°15' W

"I had everything I needed," said the forty-something-year-old. "It was time to give something back." So Sandy volunteered with Mercy Ships. She worked in the ship's reception. By day she answered phones, fielded questions, averted catastrophes. By night, she headed to the ward to spend time with her first African friend, Aminata. Only ten years separated the two women. They liked to talk and laugh. They were both independent, brave, industrious. There, though, the similarities ended. Sandy owned her own home. Aminata owned barely more than the clothes on her back. Sandy had health, financial security, many friends. Aminata was sick, indigent, friendless.

Aminata was called "the witch of Freetown" because of a tumor the size of a grapefruit growing on the side of her jaw. She lost her husband, her friends, her business in clothing retail. She turned to making money as best she could—peeling oranges for sale on the side of the street. One night she dreamed of a hospital ship that would heal her. Months later, a Mercy Ship docked in Freetown. Soon, surgeons removed Aminata's tumor and inserted a titanium jaw implant. Aminata stayed weeks onboard the ship—to Sandy's delight.

Sandy served with Mercy Ships for eight years before returning home. Ten years after she first met Aminata, Sandy made a surprise trip to Sierra Leone. One of her goals was to see Aminata again, and soon the two were laughing and talking like old times. Aminata, now reconciled with her husband, returned home, bearing gifts from Sandy. Sandy returned home convinced of three facts—friendships shape our lives; giving has its own reward; and it is possible to make a difference in a world of need.

SHIP'S LOG:
2000–2005

● ● ●

Brikama, The Gambia
13°27' N, 16°35' W

CHAPTER 12

MERCY SHIPS ON LAND AND SEA

He is no fool who gives what he cannot keep to gain what he cannot lose.

—Jim Elliott

On a street named Mercy Ships Avenue, we're in the middle of a celebration.

The nation's vice president, hundreds of villagers and local clinic workers, and crew members were all together for the daylong opening ceremony of a brand-new, just-finished HIV/AIDS clinic. And as a lasting tribute to the dedicated crew who guided it into existence, the grateful Brikama community had named the street "Mercy Ships Avenue."

Our friend, Dr. Gisela Schneider of WEC International, who'd begun an HIV/AIDS project to battle the epidemic threatening to turn Africa into a "continent of caskets"—as one UN official so graphically put it—had been treating her patients out of a storage closet, the only available space at the overcrowded Brikama Health Center.

When she heard a Mercy Ship was coming to The Gambia, Dr. Schneider contacted us, and our volunteer crew jumped at the opportunity to help. In only four months, Mercy Ships volunteers and local villagers, guided by our community development team, constructed two vitally needed buildings, one to be called the Brikama Health Clinic to teach reproductive health, the other to be a hospice.

"I have worked in Africa for a long time and can practice medicine in a hole in the ground or beneath the shade of a tree," Dr. Schneider said that day. "But now I will have running water and a sink to wash my hands in. Thank you," she said to the special crew.

If I were ever to wonder whether the Mercy Ships idea is bigger than my personal vision or touched by a providential hand, I would only have to think about the people involved and the explosion of their energy right down the gangway and onto shore.

We were already experienced in relief work and community development from the years before we began full-time hospital-ship work. These ports around the world were becoming home for our Mercy Ships, and during our months-long port stays, we had growing opportunities to work onshore. Medical and dental teams established field clinics in communities near each port city to offer local people basic health care. The more we served onshore, the more we began to see ways we might help break the cycle of poverty and disease that drove thousands to a Mercy Ship for healing and help.

Could a hospital ship charity make a lasting difference on land as well?

The volunteer dynamic of Mercy Ships seemed tailor-made for such a venture. The influx of different talents and energy and diverse skills from month to month on a Mercy Ship naturally lent itself to new ideas that extended beyond the ship itself.

So, in partnership with other humanitarian and charitable organizations, we began each year to do more and more work onshore. Immediate needs always come first, just as they do onboard the ship. Sometimes we'd help build an orphanage, other times a clinic, quite often a freshwater well or a latrine. Nobody who has ever visited a developing country can deny the immediate need and health benefits of a good, dependable latrine—not to mention the skills to build and maintain it.

Of course, the more we were involved in projects on land, the more we needed to be on land. Since the ships would ultimately sail away to other ports, we soon had a critical need for follow-ups that can be done only by trained local partners, during and after Mercy Ship port visits.

As you might imagine, we began to think deeply about what land-based projects would mean. We decided that such work would always have a Mercy Ships difference by developing an "on land" philosophy of partnerships with local people, empowering them to make a future for themselves. Whether it's building homes, digging latrines, establishing wells, or teaching health care or effective farming techniques, each project would include the education of local representatives who could train others, passing on the skills.

This had been a basic tenet of the SS *Hope,* one of our earliest inspirations for Mercy Ships. Their doctors would heal, but they'd also teach local doctors modern skills so the work could continue after the ship sailed. That's the spirit our Mercy Ships team would take with them down the gangway.

Classic thinking in the world of development says that to make a difference one must work with the big picture, the good of the many being more important than the individual. Of course, individuals such as Edoh, Tamba, Adam, Angelle, Daisy, and others you've read about in this book might strongly debate that idea.

We've decided to attempt both. A hospital ship is definitely focused on cure, but we also embrace the classic prevention idea, too. We just happen to add a Mercy Ships twist. Our focus will always be on the individual. But every group is made up of individuals, and each valued individual can serve a larger group of individuals. One person, healthy and equipped with self-sufficiency skills, has the power to change the future of his or her family. And each self-sufficient family adds to the health and welfare of its entire village. Where Mercy Ships strategically can help this happen, we will have made a lasting difference on land as well as sea.

From the Caribbean to Africa, and back again, we have already seen such partnerships work wonders.

Let me take you on a quick trip around the world with some of our land-based projects . . .

Puerto Cortes, Honduras
15°51' N, 87°57' W

Elver and the Special Nail

Gunshot and machete wounds, falls from mango trees, and injuries from hard labor provide an unending supply of battered and broken bodies to fill the orthopedic ward at each port's "poor man's hospital." ER patients lie on beds, stretchers, and on the floor, often without sheets to comfort their broken bodies. It can be overwhelming, but over and again we learn that a little can always go a long way in the developing world. The story of a boy named Elver is a good example of how it's possible to battle poverty—one family at a time.

Fifteen-year-old Elver had the sole responsibility for his family after his father went to prison. On a summer day in his high mountain village of Yoro, after he'd put in a full day constructing fences on a piece of farm-land, Elver had gone to the soccer field to have some fun. One false move later, and Elver had fractured his leg—badly. With money loaned by an uncle, Elver traveled four hours in an ambulance to the nearest medical facility. Once there, things only got worse. He stayed alone for days in the overflow ward off the emergency room, stranded, because he had no money to pay for the surgery necessary to help his leg.

Mercy Ships orthopedic surgeon Dr. Lee Zirkle was visiting the hospital during the ship's Honduras stay and met Elver. He saw that Elver's leg would never heal properly even if he could afford the surgery available. But Dr. Zirkle was convinced Elver was a good candidate for something he had designed especially for use in international orthopedic relief projects—something called a "surgical implant generation network nail." It worked. With Elver back on his feet, he could support his family again. Dr. Zirkle is a fine example of the kind of cutting-edge medical experts who volunteer to serve on a Mercy Ship. And Elver is the fine example of how meeting the needs of the one can change the future of the many.

Cotonou, Benin
6°21' N, 2°23' E

Saving the Babies

When we are invited to meet village tribal chieftains or elders, we always ask them, "What are the greatest needs you see?"

Almost invariably, the chieftain will say, "Our children and our grandchildren are our security for our old age. But so many of our babies don't live, and we don't know what causes this. Our children seem normal, and then they die."

It's true. Infant mortality is mind-boggling in sub-Saharan Africa. According to the World Health Organization's statistics for 2011, one in eight children does not live to see his fifth birthday.

The major preventative solution is so simple. Unbelievably, almost 80 percent of human illness would be eliminated from the entire planet if everyone had access to clean water and basic sanitation. Teaching basic hygiene alone can save countless babies' lives.

So, when we asked that question to the elders during our stay in Benin, we were prepared for their answer. Using creative visual methods, we explained the impact of germs to people who had never seen a microscope. We described the cycle of the hookworm and other diseases caused by poor hygiene. Mercy Ships teams have developed some very creative ways to teach this. Trust me—once you've seen the "green hand" demonstration, you'll never forget to wash your hands again.

Using a washbasin and a hand painted green to represent germs, the teachers spread that green around everywhere and to everyone with handshakes, eating, touching, and similar actions, while being unable to wash it off using only water. That simple demonstration alone has helped countless African villages become healthier.

Simple actions such as penning animals, wearing shoes, washing hands, and cleaning the water, save children's lives. With Mercy Ships' teachers-teaching-teachers philosophy of community health education, our teams pass on instruction methods such as "the green hand," so that essential health knowledge becomes part of the village's culture.

At the same time, we also build maternity-care clinics, partnering with local community leaders. Once a month, in Benin, for example, mothers can now bring their new babies into the new clinic to make sure they are healthy and up-to-date with their vaccinations. To see the joy on these mothers' faces as they hold their normal, healthy children is a special joy for us. Each healthy child is one less child in danger of dying or in need of our shipboard help.

Leon, Nicaragua
12°24' N, 86°52' W

Freetown, Sierra Leone
8°30' N, 13°15' W

Sea Legs and New Steps

Crew members often come up with brilliant solutions to the many problems we encounter. "Operation Sea Legs," for instance, was an idea that ultimately inspired our first two land programs.

Staff prosthetist Paul Moehring had a brainstorm after he created an artificial leg for a West African patient. The problem of land mines left in the aftermath of wars had begun to gain global media attention. According to one recent estimate, up to one hundred million mines remain buried in sixty-seven countries. More than one hundred thousand land mines, for example, purportedly remain buried in Nicaragua—and its civil war ended in 1990.

Children playing, farmers working their fields, innocents going about their lives, step on these mines and lose limbs. Paul believed that not only could Mercy Ships help these people with custom prosthetics, but we could build custom ones on the spot.

"Operation Sea Legs" had begun. Paul raised funds to buy an insulated forty-foot container, which he then fitted out over several years as a complete mobile prosthetic workshop able to produce an accurate and well-fitted leg within four to five hours. As soon as it was ready, we moved it to Nicaragua to respond to the need of land mine amputees there. After a while, it became apparent that physical rehabilitation alone was not enough to help amputees. Land mine casualties required sustained, long-term support services focused on helping victims earn a living and become better integrated into their communities.

So, Operation Sea Legs changed its name in 1999 to "New Steps," indicating a new direction for the program. And that direction took it toward Freetown, Sierra Leone, and the land-based program in Nicaragua broadened to encompass the support services as well as other perceived needs.

In 1999, the civil war in Sierra Leone reached the capital city, Freetown. Before the fighting was over, an estimated two thousand people in the Freetown area had lost limbs amputated by the rebel forces. Thousands more had polio, an indirect result of the war, since vaccinations ceased during the decade of conflict. Mercy Ships New Steps program started small, with a dedicated staff of only five, in January of 2000.

In April, the prosthetic container arrived.

In May, rebel forces took five hundred UN peacekeepers captive in the city. So the New Steps team was evacuated by United Nations helicopter to Guinea.

When the war finally ended, the New Steps team returned to a devastated Sierra Leone to discover that war does much more to a body than physical damage. It tears a person's heart and soul. So New Steps committed to healing lives as well as bodies, with an integrated program that provided rehabilitation, health care, and social and economic services to thousands who had been disabled and displaced by war, land mines, or disease.

Soon, New Steps was partnering with organizations such as Rotary International, Wheelchairs for the World, and the United Methodist Church to provide not only prosthetic limbs but also wheelchairs. As one woman pulled herself along the ground toward her new wheelchair, she stated, "I will never drag myself on the ground again." Once you hear something like that, you are never the same.

Molambay, Sierra Leone
8°30' N, 13°15' W

Mercy Sheep

Another example of creative thinking that gives a whole new meaning to the term "poop deck" is the "Mercy Sheep" project. In 2002, goats and sheep were purchased in The Gambia, corralled onto the aft deck of the *Anastasis*, and pampered by the crew for thirty-six hours, while sailing to Sierra Leone to replenish the livestock decimated by the country's civil war. More than 160 families in the isolated and war-devastated Molambay region outside of Freetown accepted the donated livestock and promised to donate the first female kid or lamb from the first two litters produced by their animal to a relative or neighbor, thereby helping to multiply the effort throughout the whole community.

The happy recipients of each animal had to first attend a training session with two men from the Ministry of Agriculture and a local veterinarian who helped Mercy Ships with the project. The training included the basics of proper care, feeding and watering, handling, and some information on identifying diseases. They also had to provide a shelter for their animal before receiving it and a small amount of money to cover the vaccination expenses. In 2004, Mercy Sheep volunteers hosted the country's first Sheep and Goat Show. The proud owners led their animals into an arena to view in six categories. The animals were judged and prizes awarded. The local community members decided to make the show an annual event.

Latrines, Microcredits, Swords, and Plowshares

After soldiers decimated the village of Molambay, rumors spread that these Revolutionary United Front rebels had dumped dead bodies into the clean water wells as they swept through, leaving little in their wake but destruction. Farms turned to weeds and brush; houses turned to heaps; wells turned stagnant. The people had abandoned them, running for their lives, not returning until the war's end.

The rumors of dead bodies in the wells caused the returning locals to abandon them, fearing what they might find inside. And while the Mercy Ships Water and Sanitation team never discovered evidence to prove the rumor true, they did find Molambay's wells in severe disrepair and sorely neglected. So the team taught a group of young men water and sanitation principles, including how to resurrect their dilapidated wells. Some of these same men have begun latrine-making businesses, marketing their skills to other villages to help provide for their families. With maintained latrines, fewer people will find themselves in the grip of the scourges that have been completely eliminated in the developed world.

If you believe in the value of the individual, treating people with dignity is of prime importance. So is breaking the cycle of poverty and dependence. Mercy Ships also has designed programs to give small, or microcredit, loans for individual Africans to start micro-enterprises, helping to stabilize their local economy, while giving people one more way to reclaim their own futures. The idea is to partner with people in the villages to establish "cottage" industries, jump-starting sustainable development. Some of these industries are quite remarkable.

Talk about turning swords into plowshares—men in Calaba Town, a suburb of Freetown, have turned Mercy Ships New Steps microcredit loans into the creation of some very interesting products. A talented handicapped group of war and polio victims works with Father Burton, an Italian priest famous for his rehabilitation work with ex-rebel boys. They mold cast-off brass mortar shell casings into everyday utensils as well as things of beauty, such as crosses. Their group, Handicapped Action Movement, is transforming tools of war into works of art—including handsome Mercy Ships logos—winning contracts from government, local humanitarian groups, and people in the community for their skills.

We established programs expressly for the women in the West African ports we visited. For example, along with a new dress, a new hat, and a plastic photo ID card, we give microcredit loans to women who undergo the corrective VVF surgery to help them become self-sufficient.

The Women's Initiative Program is one of these programs. Alongside other nongovernmental agencies, Mercy Ships crew members are working to help village women become leaders in their communities. I especially love the "princess project," which trains local women in commerce and cottage industries. Besides offering classes on family planning, pre- and post-natal practices, and women's health issues, the Women's Initiative also offers courses in sewing, tie-dyeing, soap-making, knitting, bookkeeping practices, and rudimentary marketing so they can market the products that they produce.

Many villages have built earthen baking ovens so that women who had no means of economic support can make a living selling bread to their own villages and to the surrounding villages as well. As of this writing, clay ovens for making bread have been built in sixteen villages and are now self-supporting, begun with funds provided by Mercy Ships. The unmistakable mouthwatering aroma of baking bread wafts throughout the village, and within hours the bread is sold out. The group shares the income among the women's families involved in the project.

Las Casitas, Nicaragua
12°42' N, 86°59' W

After Hurricanes and Coffee

Sometimes we find ourselves in the midst or aftermath of natural disasters, restoring hope and healing any way we can, as has been the case throughout our history. In 1998, not two months after the *Caribbean Mercy* crew had finished a port visit that included a medical assistance and development project at a village by the volcano Las Casitas, they were horrified to watch television coverage of Hurricane Mitch. Torrents of mud, trees, and boulders were cascading down the volcano, destroying everything in their path—a path many of the crew had recently walked. The scene resembled a moonscape; nothing was left of the homes, schools, or people in its way. The crew decided to return to help as soon as possible.

In the meantime, a small team returned to the area using any mode of transportation possible and/or feasible. Several members of the team hitched a ride on a foreign military helicopter as they made emergency food drops to communities cut off by flooding from the immense rain, then rode the rest of the way on an army truck to the mudslide area.

The scene was horrifying. Bodies were everywhere, stuck in the mudflow. Dead people, horses, and cows littered the landscape. Those who survived told the same story. The water was rising in their village. Streets were turning into small rivers. They waited inside until they heard something that sounded like helicopters coming to help them, but what they saw instead was the entire mountain coming down. Mothers told tales of their children being ripped out of their arms by the mudflow. Survivors told of being stripped naked by the force of the mud.

Amazingly enough, the mud miraculously separated and went around several of the homes of the people the *Caribbean Mercy* team had come to know, leaving intact the two wells that Mercy Ships helped the community dig. They became the only source of clean water for miles in the wake of the disaster.

The *Caribbean Mercy* soon arrived with over $2.5 million of medical supplies and medicine for the local hospitals. Cargo holds were full; the crew cabins were full. Every available space was stuffed with goods. The crew filled their backpacks with clothes and food to give away. For three days they took two trips per day to hand out supplies to the survivors. When the ship sailed, two members stayed behind to help take remaining relief supplies farther inland.

The Hurricane Mitch emergency relief run to Nicaragua was the largest-scale emergency relief undertaking in the *Caribbean Mercy's* history and led to the creation of a land-based operation in León.

An estimated 850,000 people were displaced during the hurricane, many of them permanently. The challenge was overwhelming, but our new land-based team launched into relief and longer-term development projects, working through local contacts and organizations, always keeping in mind Mercy Ships' belief in the importance of the individual. Soon, short-term volunteers arrived to begin conducting health clinics and well decontamination programs. During the six months following the hurricane, Mercy Ships Nicaragua served more than 100,000 persons in several hundred rural communities affected by the hurricane. Today, in Las Casitas, a park stands in memoriam to those who perished in the volcanic mudslide.

La Palmerita, Nicaragua
12°35' N, 86°40' W

El Tanque, Nicaragua
12°31' N, 86°57' W

Tale of Two Villages

After Hurricane Mitch, Nicaragua faced not only the same reconstruction needs we saw after the civil war in Sierra Leone, but the havoc of that incredible storm and its effects. Even periodic volcanic eruptions wreak havoc, spewing ash that kills crops and farm animals. Here, as in Africa, the fundamental objective was to partner with local people, to ultimately see them become self-sufficient, helping others to help themselves. Sometimes that meant helping two communities connect with each other.

El Tanque was a community that had to start again with nothing, having been displaced by the devastating Casita mudslide in 1998. They ultimately became completely self-sufficient, even making quite a profit on the crops they grow on their land.

La Palmerita, though, was another story. In fact, it was not even a "real" village. After many jobless and homeless farmers protested in the nation's capital, demanding help following the recent crash of the coffee industry, the Nicaraguan president granted them land to begin new lives. So 160 of these families moved to the land to create the coffee refugee community of La Palmerita.

Think about it: people from several devastated communities were suddenly thrown together to build one community where there wasn't one before. Mercy Ships helped with food distributions, construction, water and sanitation, health and agricultural projects, as best its team could, but the leaders saw that the community wouldn't be self-sufficient before the food distributions ceased.

So Mercy Ships decided to introduce the two communities—El Tanque and La Palmerita. The team set up community get-togethers to introduce the village leaders and families so neighbors could give advice to neighbors, helping each other and thereby helping themselves. And that is exactly what happened.

Katigbo, Benin
6°30' N, 2°47' E

The Place of Dying

I have seen what a transformation such efforts can make, with my own eyes, in only a matter of years. The transformation can be literally from death to life.

In Benin, along what is known as the "old slave coast," is an area called Katigbo. It has one of the highest infant mortality rates, lowest life expectancies, and worst economic conditions of the entire nation, and it has been known for hundreds of years as "the place of the dying"—the literal meaning of the word *Katigbo*.

Not too far away is "The Road of No Return," and at its end stands the monument to the old slave-gathering castle, where captured slaves would be made to walk seven times around the castle's tree, which by legend would make the new slaves forget their past, dying to their previous lives of freedom.

As I drove along the road to Katigbo in 1998, I saw all sorts of cottage industries based around the woodworking of beautiful native teak, rosewood, and other exotic hardwoods. But what they were making were coffins—ornate, hand-carved coffins. Their beauty was heart-stopping. I saw one that looked like the head of a rooster, another like an airplane; the creativity seemed to know no bounds. Soon I learned this was Katigbo's main industry—the building of coffins. Its people spent more money for the coffin and burial ceremony for their loved ones than they would have spent on them during the entire rest of their lives.

As I gazed at all this, I realized why. Death was still everywhere. Long after the slave trade was gone, people were still dying, but now the deaths were from rampant disease, malnutrition, and horrid economic conditions. Death was a major part of the culture. There was a pervasive lack of hope to change anything for the better, so the mourning was constant—from cradle to certain, quick grave. They knew no other way but death. It became their culture in a way we can never quite understand.

In the months ahead, along with local partnerships and with the aid of other nongovernmental groups in the country, Mercy Ships teams went into the villages along this road and began to work to break this cycle. We began to teach basic health care and hygiene lessons and to teach suitable students how to teach others these basics. We partnered with them to build a maternity clinic to help decrease the death rate for mothers and babies.

Their land was fertile, but the villagers starved half the year, because they had no way of storing grain. So Mercy Ships teams partnered with the village leaders to build their own granaries. We helped with design and oversight; they built it, and they owned it. After the ship departed, the Beninois students trained by Mercy Ships in a district called Ifangni, fifty-five miles from Cotonou, formed a registered nongovernmental organization called "D4D Anastasis."

D4D stands for development in four dimensions—the spiritual, social, intellectual, and physical. Now under their own initiative, D4D developed plans to build a community center and grain storage facility to house grain during the non-growing season so their communities can counter the malnourishment their children suffer during the lean months. They pool funds and purchase grain in quantity at the lowest prices during the harvest season, sell the grain back to their community with a small surcharge to cover costs, and, by doing so, they have seen a small profit as well as broken the cycle of malnutrition and poverty. After we sailed, we heard that the group was planning a water tower and had organized plans for construction and financing, entirely on their own.

Five years later, I returned to Benin. As I drove along the same Katigbo road, I found myself speechless at the change I saw. The main enterprise along the road was still woodworking, using the wonderful, exotic woods all ornately, beautifully crafted—but the products were now beds, chairs, tables, and furniture—things for the living.

What had changed?

There is now less death, so perhaps there is less money to be made in coffins and more money to be made in expressing their talents through things of beauty for the living.

And even better, there was now a future—of their own making.

Irbil, Iraq
36°11' N, 44°01' E

Columbus, Ohio
39°59' N, 82°59' W

Into Other Lands

The volunteer flood down our gangway is flowing ever outward. In small but significant ways, we've begun to look for chances to partner in new areas of the world. In 2003, for instance, we joined a coalition of 173 other organizations and the United Nations in a massive operation to help Iraq after the overthrow of Saddam Hussein's government. Operation Iraqi Mercy was a collaborative effort with our partner German relief agency, Humedica, that served thousands of people with practical assistance and promoted a message of reconciliation and friendship.

The team found four Kurdish children with conditions they couldn't cure there. So the team made a major commitment to provide them with the medical aid they needed. The two girls, ages nine and five, suffering from serious congenital heart defects, were flown with their fathers to Ohio. The other two, young brothers, ages five and six, were victims of a land mine explosion. One lost his left arm, and both boys suffered severe shrapnel wounds to the eyes.

In Ohio, a former Mercy Ships eye surgeon volunteer had enlisted his colleagues' expertise in an attempt to save them. Everyone waived fees, Mercy Ships paid traveling expenses, the Kurdish Humanitarian Rights Watch assisted in obtaining humanitarian parole visas, and Airserv evacuated all four children and parents for free from Iraq to Jordan. Royal Jordanian Airlines offered a discount for the U.S. portion of the flights.

And a whole merciful army of Ohioans pulled together to support the children's medical visit.

These and hundreds of other such Mercy Ships stories only happen because of the generous donors financially supporting the work and because of the almost one thousand volunteer crew and students from more than fifty countries who give time every year to offer their skills, talent, energy, and hearts to make it so.

Longitude/Latitude: From Everywhere

Admirals of Mercy

Who are these people who serve with Mercy Ships?

On a hospital ship, the medical work of healing the thousands who stream up our gangway is what gets most of the outward attention. In reality, that is only about 40 percent of the actual work that makes a ship "go." The 60 percent behind the scenes is what fuels the medical miracles on land and sea. Mercy Ships could not happen without every one of them.

Crew on the ships at any one time represent dozens of different nations—multicultural, multiethnic, multitalented.

English is the common language, and Catholic or Protestant Christianity in all its denominational variations—orthodox, mainline, evangelical, charismatic—is the predominant faith. There are also volunteers who have no religious persuasion, but want to help make the world a better place to live.

Professional deckhands from both developed and developing nations keep the ships shipshape. We have had a physical therapist from Portugal; an agricultural specialist from the United States; and a professional dancer from Trinidad, once recognized on the London dance scene, was our media relations expert for most of our first twenty-five years.

A judge from the federal court in San Diego, California, has volunteered twice to be the ship's "storesman." He carries the "stores" from where they are kept in cold and dry storage two decks below the galley, up the stairs and into the galley.

A blood relative of the queen of England was part of our crew for five different visits to Africa. She was a part of the remarkable hospice team who visited those we could not help. The hospice team counseled the families on terminal care, not only bringing medical materials they could not afford, but also offering those individuals a greater dignity for the final months of their lives and peace in the midst of tragedy.

Her service, along with others who continue to do hospice care, has made one of the greatest statements Mercy Ships could make about the value of life—that the way we end our lives is important.

We have volunteers who have had their own lives transformed by the surgeries we specialize in—a nurse who had pediatric cornea transplant surgery, a ship's officer who endured cleft lip and palate surgeries throughout his life. A woman from a long line of seafarers signed on as a third mate. A shipyard manager for an atomic submarine manufacturer became an executive officer. A teacher from England guided our multifaceted on-land operation.

We've had cooks from Norway, the United States, Ghana, and the Netherlands. And everyone onboard a ship knows that a crew's goodwill is directly proportional to the food they eat. If you have a good cook, you have a happy ship. If you don't have a good cook, you don't have a happy ship. So those who prepare the food, who wash the dishes, and who clean and do the service industry activities are a pivotal part of what makes Mercy Ships International stay happily afloat.

They come from everywhere and every background, every ethnicity and nationality, even from other, stranded, ships. A Jamaican engineer was on a Russian ship in Mexican water when the Russian ship went into bankruptcy. The crew onboard the ship were hungry. They couldn't go ashore because they were not Mexican citizens, so our crew, while we were in Lazaro Cardenas, began to help the crew stuck onboard. The Jamaican engineer asked if he could transfer to the Mercy Ship. We made arrangements with the agent ashore, and he joined us.

Our very first captain was a former Navy seal and a master mariner. Another of our captains was helping load equipment from his ship onto the *Caribbean Mercy. This is something I would like to do with the rest of my life. I would love to raise my family onboard a ship,* he thought, after finding out more about us. And soon he and his family joined the crew.

The school onboard is one of the great strengths. The school on the *Anastasis*, for instance, had more than fifty students and at least seven full-time teachers, who meet during regular school-day hours. One of our educators was a teacher at one of England's most prestigious private schools.

From my perspective, the families who bring their children to serve onboard a Mercy Ship provide their children an educational experience with an exposure to the globe unmatched by any university degree program. The geography, the people, the languages, the cultures, and the economic systems they see on a daily basis are unparalleled. I've seen the effect on my own children, who have gone into their adult lives with an awareness of the world they could never have had through a conventional childhood on land.

I have always gathered people around me who were smarter than I am. In certain areas I think our organization is close to genius. I am continually awed by the wonder-working gifts of the kind of person who becomes a ship's engineer. Watching one fix an average day's crises would convince anyone of that. But the same goes for anyone who chooses Mercy Ships as a career. Every one of our career volunteers seem able to do almost anything and actually looks for chances to do so—even our doctors.

Dr. Gary Parker has not only served as the Chief Medical Officer in Mercy Ships, but also served as Executive Director of the *Anastasis. (see photo 4)* Yet that wasn't enough for this man. Case in point: While coming out of port in the Dominican Republic, not too long before we sailed to Africa in 1990, the *Anastasis* ran aground. This 11,701-ton ship was stuck, the propellers embedded in a coral reef behind us and in land in front of us. The propellers, by the way, even with the engines off, move with wave action. Since we were concerned that we were going to do even more serious damage to our propellers by forcing our way back into safe waters, someone had to go down and clear the path.

Who volunteered to don his scuba gear and clear the coral away from those massive but delicate propellers which the waves are moving at will? Dr. Gary Parker, whose hands should be insured for several million dollars, used those hands to get the ship sailing again. That tells you something about the kind of people who choose to spend a large part of their lives onboard a Mercy Ship.

As one Maritime Academy graduate has put it, "Mercy Ships is more than the sea, and much more than just a job. It's my life."

The sky is the limit; the sea is the road.

Mercy Ships staff and crew, those who have made Mercy Ships a career, are truly a rare group. From doctors to deck hands, everyone onboard pays his or her own way for the privilege of serving the poor. How is this done?

Crew raise their own support. A short-term crew member volunteers from two weeks to one year, either aboard ship or in one of our land-based offices. Crew range from eighteen-year-olds to retirees. Long-term crew members make a two-year commitment or longer. For those who make Mercy Ships a career, most of them raise their own financial support. For example, Dr. Gary Parker, who came to help our efforts after the 1986 Mexico City earthquake for two weeks and has been with us ever since, asked his home church to sponsor him on that Mexico trip, and they are still sponsoring him today.

I am convinced that this dynamic also fosters a real camaraderie, an *esprit de corps,* that goes beyond the people who actually get to be on the ship to those who support those who do. That's a powerful thing. And it's been a strong, quiet force in our success and in the deep sense of fulfillment that is the hallmark of Mercy Ships.

Becoming a "Shipmate" of Mercy Ships is how thousands of people join Mercy Ships without leaving home. These are people who believe in what we are doing and pledge to help keep Mercy Ships afloat, giving to us, as a charity, in the traditional way.

I've noticed a great dynamic at work in many of our volunteer crew and staff. Some were clearly on a pathway for success until they realized they wanted to do something more than become "successful." So they took a turn onto the pathway of significance beyond success and found their way to us. The success/significance transition is a big one in the world today—the desire for legacy is a strong urge.

Actually, there is a theme of legacy throughout the whole Mercy Ships story, beginning with the Italian maritime leader who sold us the *Victoria,* which became the *Anastasis,* for a rock-bottom price. From the various captains, to the executive directors, to the able-bodied seaman, everyone involved with Mercy Ships is here for reasons having to do with leaving a meaningful legacy.

But surprisingly enough, the rewards come along the way. And sometimes they meet you at the door. Dr. Keith Thomson, a consultant anesthetist from the U.K., experienced this in a fascinating way. During a visit to a maternity hospital in Sierra Leone as a volunteer, Dr. Thomson found a nineteen-year-old woman in severe distress in the labor ward.

"What's wrong with this woman?" he asked the midwives.

The answer: "She has been in labor for four days, and she doesn't have the money for the Caesarian section that she needs."

"Well, what will happen to her?" he asked.

The answer: "She will probably die."

"If I pay, will you do the surgery?" he asked.

The midwives asked the surgeon, who asked for a 20 percent deposit of the total amount—the equivalent of one hundred dollars.

Dr. Thomson paid it. The Caesarian section was performed, and a lovely little baby girl was born.

Five years later, Dr. Thomson arrived at Conakry, Guinea's airport, to rejoin the *Anastasis*. As he left the airplane, he saw a couple with a child holding up a sign that said: "Welcome, Uncle Keith. Thank you for saving my life and my mom's life. You are most welcome!"

Who are these people who have spent from two weeks to a lifetime to keep this dream of Mercy Ships afloat for a quarter of a century? Who have poured down our gangways to take fresh ideas, stubborn energy, and optimism into the lives of others—beyond all logic, beyond all statistics, beyond all reason and doubt?

They are committed individuals with varied skill sets, who have found a meaningful way to share their blessings. They share important characteristics—compassion, patience, flexibility, and perseverance.

Following the model of Jesus, the volunteers who fuel the Mercy Ships programs reflect that overflow of energy and heart and desire to put love into action. We exist today, and we face a bright future tomorrow, because of them.

And we are, with small steps, with new steps, making a lasting difference, one person at a time.

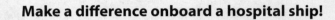
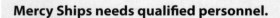

SHIP'S LOG: 2007

● ● ●

Newcastle, England
55° 02' N, 01° 42' W

Rotterdam, Holland
51° 55' N, 4° 30' E

Canary Islands
28° 18' N, 16° 34' W

CHAPTER 13

THE *AFRICA MERCY* MAKES ITS DEBUT

A leader, once convinced that a particular course of action is the right one, must . . . be undaunted when the going gets tough.

—Ronald Reagan

Between the conception and the birth of the *Africa Mercy* were eight very long years. Transforming a Danish rail ferry into a world-class hospital ship was the largest conversion project of its kind in the UK. Like most construction projects, this one was plagued by labor and construction delays. The year 2005 came and went without the planned launch. Then 2006 followed suit.

On April 6, 2006, as construction crews continued work on the *Africa Mercy* below decks, Mercy Ships supporters and crew gathered for a special commissioning service in anticipation of the ship's upcoming deployment to Africa. British House of Lords member and Mercy Ships UK Board Chairman, Lord Ian McColl, served as host for the event. Dame Norma Major, wife of former British Prime Minister John Major, presided over the ceremony. Mercy Ships International Board Chairman Mike Ullman gave the opening prayer.

Special guest Madame Kartumu Boakai, wife of the newly-elected Vice President of Liberia, brought warm greetings from the Liberian people and best wishes from Liberian President Ellen Johnson Sirleaf. Noting that the *Africa Mercy* was scheduled to visit Liberia, Madame Boakai said, "Something good is about to happen!"

Finally, after eight years and $62 million (approximately £30 million), the fourth ship to be operated by Mercy Ships was finished—and she was a beauty! The *Africa Mercy* was so large that all three of our previous ships could fit inside it with room to spare. The ship's 8 decks contained 6 operating theaters, a 78-bed hospital ward, 474 berths for crew, an x-ray room, a CT scanner, a pharmacy, and schoolroom to accommodate up to 60 students.

When we started Mercy Ships nearly 30 years ago, we never dreamed the organization would become so significant . . . or that we would have such a fine hospital ship to serve the world's poor. It had taken a lot of perseverance—which I've decided is one of the most important leadership qualities—but it had been a privilege every step of the way.

I thought of all of the people who had contributed to this moment. Fundraising efforts had taken place all over the world. This was the most ambitious project ever undertaken by Mercy Ships—and each donor, each worker, each person who prayed were a part of the mercy that would be delivered by this ship.

Every ship has life savers, but the *Africa Mercy* itself is a life saver for the poorest of the poor—people who are living lives of desperation with no hope in sight. But when this huge hospital ship docks in an African port, it is a symbol of hope, love, and mercy.

The *Africa Mercy* had to clear one more hurdle before it could begin its mission. It had to successfully complete its sea trials. The sea trials took place in the North Sea under the supervision of Bureau Veritas, the French international marine certification organization. The trials took approximately 24 hours, in which all systems onboard were checked.

Ten days later, on March 29, 2007, the loudspeaker onboard the *Africa Mercy* made the announcement we had all been waiting for—the world's largest hospital ship had passed its sea trials and was ready for service! A palpable relief swept through a Mercy Ships reception as the task was completed.

Of course, many others shared my relief and joy. Mike Ullman, Chairman of Mercy Ships International, said, "This is a momentous day for everyone involved in Mercy Ships. Hundreds of people have worked tirelessly on this project, and we owe each of them a huge debt."

Ann Gloag, the UK-based philanthropist, said, "When I originally put up the first donation to buy the ferry, I knew it would be a long, tough project, and it certainly has been. However, when you consider that this ship used to be a rail ferry and is now a state-of-the-art hospital ship, all the hard work has been well worthwhile."

Lord Ian McColl, Chairman of Mercy Ships UK and Vice-Chair of Mercy Ships International, said, "This is a truly momentous day for Mercy Ships. I have worked as a volunteer surgeon on many occasions with Mercy Ships, and I am very much looking forward to working on this purposely converted state-of-the-art hospital ship. The life-changing operations that we undertake are so common practice in developed countries but are simply not available to the poorest people in Africa."

The next step was to load the ship with over $2 million (£1 million) worth of hospital supplies, equipment, and materials. Additional essential items were also loaded, including 3000 rolls of toilet paper (a 3-month supply), 400 wastepaper bins, 26.8 tons of frozen meat and fish (a 4-month supply), 420kg of coffee (courtesy of Starbucks), and 4000kg of breakfast cereal. The vessel was literally transformed into a hospital and a small village.

Finally, the preparations were complete. As I anticipated the ship's inaugural sail to Africa—with stops in Rotterdam, Holland, and in the Canary Islands—all of the frustrations and uncertainties of the past eight years seem to fade in the light of the future's promise.

On May 4, 2007, the *Africa Mercy* began its inaugural sail from England. Its first stop was Rotterdam, Holland, for the ship's official introduction to the media. It was a gala event that included tours of the ship, interviews, and informational meetings with various media representatives. In line with his company's emphasis on corporate social responsibility, Mr. Hans ten Cate, Chairman of Rabobank Netherlands, presented a check to Mercy Ships for EUR 14,000—the operational cost of one day on the *Africa Mercy*.

On May 8th, the *Africa Mercy* began its six-day sail toward its next stop, the Canary Islands, off the northwest coast of Africa. The realities of sailing on a flat-bottomed former rail ferry quickly became apparent. The first part of the sail, through the English Channel, was a bit bumpy. But as the ship reached the Bay of Biscay, the ride became quite a test for the landlubbers onboard. (I was most grateful that my schedule did not allow for me to sail on this particular trip!)

The winds increased in ferocity, reaching gale force 10 (on a Beaufort scale of 1–12), causing the waves to swell from 8 feet to 12 feet. Fortunately, the *Africa Mercy* is a very stable ship and rights herself quickly—a quickness that makes the ride even more interesting.

The ship came through the storm strong and safe. Unfortunately, the same could not be said for some of the breakable items that were not stored correctly! All in all, it was an inaugural sail to remember! One philosophical crew member said he "would take this sail any day over being moored to the dock." I couldn't agree more!

After crossing the Bay of Biscay, the sea became calm, and the remainder of the sail was lovely. As the ship neared Tenerife in the Canary Islands, crew members shed their coats and jackets and gathered on "Monkey Island" (top of the bridge) to enjoy the sunshine and the beautiful blue ocean.

The ship arrived safely in beautiful Tenerife for refueling and for divers to check the bottom of the ship for the surveyors. The crew enjoyed a day off to enjoy the culture.

Now the *Africa Mercy* was ready to begin its intended purpose—delivering hope and healing to the world's forgotten poor."

Next stop: LIBERIA!

SHIP'S LOG:
2007–2008

● ● ●

Monrovia, Liberia
06° 18' N, 10° 42' W

CHAPTER 14

NEW SHIP, NEW PRESIDENT, NEW HOPE

My mandate was to return hope to the country and to make the children smile again.

—Her Excellency, Madame President Ellen
Johnson Sirleaf, Liberia

Liberia . . . ravaged by civil war
. . . brave in its poverty
. . . rising from the ashes

The Ducor Palace Hotel sat like a ghostly sentinel—on a hill overlooking Monrovia, the capital city of Liberia. The once opulent five-star hotel had 300 rooms, a pool, tennis courts, and a French restaurant. But then a struggle for political power turned into 14 years of devastating civil war. The hotel was destroyed by violence and looting. Now it is a concrete shell, wearing the shabby vestiges of its former glory with a quiet dignity. It is an apt symbol for the country of Liberia.

On January 16, 2006, Ellen Johnson Sirleaf was inaugurated as the President of Liberia—the very first democratically elected female president of an African nation. She inherited a country with terrible physical and emotional damage from a decade-long brutal civil war. Now it was one of the poorest countries on earth. The economy was in shambles. The medical infrastructure was virtually destroyed. There was no national telephone service, electrical grid, or piped water. The country's new president declared her intention to return hope to a country that desperately needed it—an intention shared by Mercy Ships.

In May, the *Africa Mercy* arrived in Monrovia, joining its sister ship, the *Anastasis. (see photo 10)* The crews of both ships were officially and warmly welcomed by President Ellen, as the Liberian women fondly call her, who said, "All of you who serve on this ship and serve voluntarily, the Liberian people receive you with such warmth, just knowing what you bring . . . what you bring to us. How you enable us—many of our people—to live again. To be able to become a part of society in a normal way. No longer an object of pity. No longer silenced by their handicaps. No longer ashamed of their condition. We thank you."

The Passing of the Torch

After 25 years of service as a symbol of hope in over 275 ports, it was time for the graceful lady of the sea, the *Anastasis*, to retire. Crew members worked long hours to move vital equipment and supplies from the *Anastasis* to the *Africa Mercy*.

As the Passing of the Torch ceremony began, I looked across to the *Anastasis*, and my mind was flooded by memories and images. Nearly 30 years of history lay before me—a multitude of wonders that God had performed through our dedicated crew. Docked side-by-side, the *Anastasis* and the *Africa Mercy* represented the old and the new, the past and the future. This special day was a celebration of both.

From the top of the gangway on the *Africa Mercy*, I faced a spectacular sight. Winding from one ship to the other was a colorful array of Mercy Ships crew and board members—representing all ages and 35 different nationalities. And they stood together, in unity, to celebrate the passing of the torch.

Beginning the ceremony on the opposite gangway, Dr. Gary Parker raised an iron cross high above his head. It had been welded to the bow-sprit on the *Anastasis*. This hand-made cross welded in the midst of a crest was passed from one hand to the next, until it reached Deyon's and my hands on the new ship. That same cross will lead us at the bow of the *Africa Mercy*.

After the cross, the torch followed—appropriately constructed from materials from all of the ships. The torch was crafted from teak from the *Caribbean Mercy*, an oil separator sleeve from the *Anastasis,* and a small wooden cross from the lignum vitae wood main shaft bearing on the *Good Samaritan* (*Island Mercy*).

As I stood watching, I remembered other lines—the lines at medi-cal screening days, lines that can stretch as far as one can see, lines filled with thousands of desperate, and yet wonderful, people who needed the life-changing surgeries Mercy Ships offers. *(see photo 1)*

Nearly two million people had been transformed by the work of Mercy Ships. As we committed the *Africa Mercy* to the future, I stood in awe of a God who is always faithful, supporters who believe in our vision and purpose, and a multinational crew to serve even more of the world's forgotten poor as we all follow the 2000-year-old model of Jesus of Nazareth.

Mercy Ships Returns to Liberia

The enormous challenge of rebuilding a nation after the long and devas-tating civil war in Liberia prompted Mercy Ships to return to that coun-try for its 2008 Field Service. According to the WHO Global Health Observatory Data Repository, the country had only four dentists and 51 doctors to care for the 3.3 million people, and many of the hospitals had been destroyed or made inoperable by two decades of civil war. President Sirleaf personally requested the return of the hospital ship, saying, "The *Africa Mercy* offers an indispensable bridge by responding to individual medical crises."

And Mercy Ships did return and set a new record in the number of people served. One of the patients whose life was transformed was a little girl named Blessing.

Blessing was a normal, active nine-year-old. As she was walking home from school one day, she fell into a ditch and wounded her left leg. The wound became infected. Doctors at the local hospital diagnosed the infection as noma, a flesh-destroying bacteria. Noma is a disease of poverty—resulting from malnutrition, a weakened immune system, and little access to common drugs, such as penicillin, which can cure this horrible bacteria. The West has seen noma only in concentration camps during World War II, where malnutrition was prevalent and sanitation was woefully absent.

The relentless bacteria attacked the soft flesh around Blessing's mouth, destroying the tissue—eating away her lips and nose—and causing excruciating pain. At that point, someone referred Blessing to Mercy Ships. Volunteer surgeons took a skin graft from her upper thigh and applied it to the damaged area of her knee. Then two layers of skin were attached to her neck and cultured for the next surgery. During the second operation, these flaps of skin were used to reconstruct Blessing's lips and part of her nose.

It was a difficult time for Blessing. The disease and the treatment were painful. When she became discouraged, her father (the pastor of a local church) and her mother would assure her that it was all necessary for her to get well and have a "normal" life again.

Their words were true. Each week Blessing's condition improved. Her mother praised God for her daughter's recovery and for the free world-class medical care. She said, "I continually thank God for His goodness toward us, as my husband and I were not in any position to afford the treatment needed by our daughter."

Today, Blessing is a joyful, confident girl who wins the hearts of all who meet her. She is an inspiration—and a blessing—to others, although she will carry the scars of noma for the rest of her life.

In addition to providing immediate medical care, Mercy Ships also helped in building medical infrastructure and community development that would help the people of Liberia long after the ship left port. These efforts in capacity building encompassed training, construction projects, and agricultural projects.

Medical training was offered in many areas. Mercy Ships anesthetist Dr. Keith Thomson, from the UK, held a three-day conference on anesthesia at the JFK Hospital in Monrovia. Training for lab technicians, biomedical technicians, community health workers, and mental health workers was also provided. Local nurses and doctors were given specialized instruction in care and surgical techniques for ophthalmic problems and obstetric fistula repair.

One of the particularly remarkable capacity-building projects was the restoration of two wards in the JFK Hospital to their pre-war condition. One ward was funded by the Gloag Foundation of Scottish philanthropist Ann Gloag, and Mercy Ships provided funding for the second. We also provided consultation and monitored the progress of this endeavor. As an expression of the country's appreciation, President Sirleaf admitted Mrs. Gloag into the Order of the Star of Africa with the grade of Commander.

A conversation I had with President Sirleaf resulted in another capacity-building project. She told me about her frustrating search to find someone to rebuild the clinic in Tenegar (near her ancestral home) and we were able to complete the ***Tenegar Clinic . . . "Hope on the Hill."***

The clinic was almost destroyed during Liberia's long civil war. Then a joint effort of Mercy Ships and the local community rebuilt it.

You could feel the excitement in the crowd as they waited—some for over 5 hours. Hundreds of people from the community and neighboring villages had come to celebrate. Most were wearing traditional Liberian dress or their very best clothes. People were singing and dancing. The scene was set for the arrival of President Ellen to dedicate the newly reconstructed Tenegar clinic, as she had spent her childhood nearby. Not only was President Ellen a national hero, but she was also a hero in her home community as well!

Finally, President Ellen arrived, and the ceremony began. Ken Berry, Managing Director of the *Africa Mercy*, praised the community of Tenegar for their part in the reconstruction, saying, "You—the men and women of this community—banded together to help ensure your future and that of generations to come."

The Liberian Minister of Health and Social Welfare, Dr. Walter Gwenigale, stressed the importance of an organization that "follows the model of Jesus" being willing to build a clinic in a Muslim community. He said, "I am very pleased that this Christian ship did not say, 'No, we will not serve Muslims.'"

President Ellen addressed the crowd, saying, "When we got the message that Mercy Ships would do the clinic, what a wonderful day it was!" Then she cut the ribbon that stretched across the clinic's doorway, officially completing the dedication.

The word *tenegar* means "on the hill." This new clinic "on the hill" will be a beacon of hope and healing, as it will serve over 6000 people in the surrounding area—people without access to adequate health care.

Royesville . . . A Community Transformed by Forgiveness

Royesville, an area made up of over 15 villages, was the site of another Mercy Ships capacity-building project. During Liberia's long civil war, the roads and bridges connecting these villages to the main road were destroyed. Now, they are only accessible by foot—walking over a bamboo footbridge and hiking 30 minutes through the bush.

Mercy Ships volunteers Jean-Claude and Anastasie wanted to start a community development farm in the Royesville area. To introduce the project, they invited the villagers to a meal.

But the people refused to sit together. They huddled in groups according to their villages. For many years, they had been divided by civil war and ethnic conflicts.

Jean-Claude pointed to his wife and then asked the group, "Where shall **we** eat? We do not belong to your village?"

There was silence. Finally, one of the chiefs stood and said, "God has brought these people to help us. We must work together."

People began to ask for forgiveness. People offered forgiveness. Walls were broken down.

The people began to work, sweat, and laugh together as they learned better, more efficient farming methods. The community farm produced cabbage, corn, collard greens, pineapples, peanuts, and nutritious moringa tree leaves.

The people named the community project "God's Gift." Thomas Walker, a chief in one of the villages, explained, "Mercy Ships was the first group to come across the broken bridge to help us. We say that only someone who has God's love can do that!"

One day as Thomas walked with the Mercy Ships team back to the main road, he pointed to the logo on the side of the Mercy Ships vehicle. He observed, "It's true what it says on your truck. Mercy Ships does bring hope and healing."

The community development project has truly been "God's Gift" to the people of Royesville . . . in many ways, and for years to come.

Saying Farewell to Liberia

During the many months in Liberia, the country's people and their president touched our hearts. It was a bittersweet moment when the time came for the *Africa Mercy* to leave Monrovia. President Ellen Johnson Sirleaf, accompanied by the country's Vice-President and Mrs. Joseph Boakai, visited the ship to express their gratitude to the crew, to acknowledge the investment made by Mercy Ships in their country, and to pledge that progress would continue.

Madame Kartumu Boakai had visited our International Operations Center in Texas to learn more about Mercy Ships and spent time in our home. We found Madame Boakai to exemplify all that is good of this nation that was founded by West Africans who returned to African shores after the U.S. War of Independence.

President Sirleaf noted, "You've touched the lives of Liberians who could not be reached by their own government because of the lack of resources—human, financial, technical."

She went on to say, "We have lot of partners—bilateral, multilateral, private partners. And many of them have so many more resources to give us. They talk about $200 million agreements . . . but $11 million [the Mercy Ships estimated financial investment in 2008], I dare say, has touched lives much more than these. You see, it's not so much the size of the assistance and the magnitude of the resources. It is what comes with it . . . whom it touches . . . whom it reaches . . . whom it changes . . . that is what true partnership is all about, and I want to thank you!

"I don't know where you go next, but I do know the country which you now move on to serve will also be blessed by the things you have done. They are our neighbors. So we'll continue to benefit from that service. Because a strong Liberia or a strong Benin or a strong Togo or a strong Cote d'Ivoire or a strong Sierra Leone also makes a strong West Africa, and that's good for us."

And, after a brief stay for regular maintenance in the Canary Islands, the *Africa Mercy* headed for its next West African port—Cotonou, Benin—with a firm determination to leave even more footprints of mercy.

SHIP'S LOG:
2009–2010

●●●

Cotonou, Benin
06° 21' N, 02° 23' E

Lomé, Togo
06° 10' N, 01° 21' E

CHAPTER 15

LEAVING FOOTPRINTS OF MERCY

Let us be sure that those who come after will say of us in our time, that in our time we did everything that could be done.

—Ronald Reagan

In February 2009 the *Africa Mercy* arrived in the port of Cotonou for the fourth Mercy Ships visit to Benin. Unlike the surrounding African countries, Benin has been blessed with peace for many years. Its basic infrastructure—power, water, buildings—is sound. However, it lacks modern equipment, supplies, and technical training. Health care is extremely limited and unaffordable for the majority of the population.

Two unique aspects of the Benin Field Service increased our impact. First, to make our surgical procedures more accessible, medical screenings were held in two locations in the northern portion of the country—in addition to the screenings in the Cotonou area. Second, we established a Hospitality Center in a building located just two blocks from the ship. It was a comfortable place for patients to gain stamina prior to surgery and for patients to stay while undergoing follow-up treatment after surgery. As a result, the beds in the onboard hospital ward were more quickly available—which translated into more surgeries performed and more people helped.

While the Benin Field Service eclipsed all previous records in the number of people served, we were also determined to leave footprints of mercy in Benin in order to meet future needs long after the *Africa Mercy* left the country. Our efforts to build infrastructure focused on training, community development projects, and construction projects.

The *Africa Mercy* provides an effective platform for offering training to African health care providers. Alcon, a division of Novartis, provided a $50,000 grant for capacity building and opportunity to offer Alcon-Mercy Ships Fellowships for qualified surgeons. Both Togolese and Beninese ophthalmologists participated. They learned a sutureless cataract surgery technique—a method developed specifically for the very dense cataracts created by the intense African sun and the lack of preventative eye care. Dr. Glenn Strauss explained, "The Beninese surgeons have been about 15 or 20 years behind what's happening in the rest of the world. I was able to introduce a procedure that is appropriate for the technology that they have, that is within the scope of what they can accomplish here. They were thrilled! In fact, one of the surgeons commented to me, 'This is going to change eye surgery in Benin for years to come!'"

One of the five ophthalmic surgeons from Benin who received training was Dr. Ogbe Barikissou, a local surgeon from Porto-Novo. She is the Director of the National Eye Care Program for Benin. When she received an invitation to meet with Mercy Ships, she was skeptical. She had previously sat through many meetings with well-intended relief workers. She thought, "Okay, here goes . . . another NGO needing to be babysat and watched over." She wondered how much of her time they would require.

But, when Dr. Ogbe met with Dr. Glenn, she was not only surprised—she was excited and invigorated by the training we were offering! She and two of her team members participated in the training. Previously, at the Porto-Novo Hospital, they had performed less than 100 cataract removals in an entire year. At the end of their training with Mercy Ships, they were performing 58 surgeries per week, increasing their annual capacity by over 500%! Dr. Ogbe is now doing cataract surgery on her own . . . and training other doctors. She said, "Mercy Ships, you have completely changed my perspective. Mercy Ships came to us. And instead of US serving YOU . . . YOU came to serve US!"

Dr. Wendy Hofman completed the three-month Alcon fellowship onboard the *Africa Mercy*. Afterward, she went to rural Gabon where she will work with the medical arm of Samaritan's Purse. She will practice ophthalmology at Bongolo Hospital, a rural mission hospital run by the Christian Missionary Alliance, and she will be the only eye doctor within a 350-mile radius.

Half of the blindness in Africa is caused by cataracts. Many children are born with congenital cataracts. One of the most dramatic stories of restored sight is that of Genevieve's three children.

Darkness Lifting

Genevieve's three children lived in a personal darkness because they were born with cataracts. They lived in a world of subtle shifts in light and shadow. Going anywhere was an exercise in patience and vigilance. Genevieve tied one-year-old Ricardo on her back with a piece of brightly-patterned cloth, took seven-year-old Alexis by the hand, and held three-year-old Nadege by the arm. She guided them up steps, through doorways, and around potholes.

Genevieve was literally her children's eyes—on the alert for common dangers, such as coal stoves and containers of hot liquid. She said, *"Because of the blindness, I must be with them all the day. Even if they are playing, I have to watch them. In everything, I have to be right beside them."*

The emotional strain was almost unbearable. What would become of her children in a country that makes no accommodations for blindness? And the despair was deepened by cruel whispers. People said that the blindness was caused by witchcraft. And even Genevieve wondered, *"What did I do to God for this to happen?"*

Then a glimmer of hope began to penetrate the darkness when André, a man from their village, offered to help. He heard about Mercy Ships on the radio and arranged transportation and housing for Genevieve's family.

Arriving at the ship was a great adventure for the children. They laughed, played, and mimicked the foreign noises of the ship.

But Genevieve was nervous—daring to hope, yet afraid of disappointment.

On the Thursday before Easter, the Mercy Ships eye team performed the cataract removal surgeries. The children spent the night with their eyes covered by patches.

The next morning, the big moment arrived—it was time to remove the bandages! Three-year-old Nadege was first. She proved she could see when she grabbed a doll and said, "Bébé, bébé."

Next was seven-year-old Alexis. He looked around and then walked confidently over to Dr. Glenn.

At first, Baby Ricardo kept his eyes squeezed tightly shut. Finally, he opened one eye, and then both eyes. He glanced around. Suddenly, he noticed something on his mother's shirt and reached up and grabbed it.

All three of Genevieve's children could see! Now they could see their parents' faces for the first time. Now they could go to school. Now they could go outside to play.

Genevieve simply said, *"I am so happy. I cannot tell you how happy I am."*

Darkness and despair were gone! Light and hope had come! Mercy Ships literally follows the 2000-year-old model of Jesus!

A Celebration of Sight

After having cataracts removed, eye patients return for a procedure known as a YAG laser treatment. This procedure prevents a film-like layer from developing over the lens and impeding vision.

Once the YAG treatment is complete, patients join together for a time of singing, dancing, and thanksgiving. It is a Celebration of Sight! Can you imagine over 100 people, who have been blind for years, gathered in a room to celebrate the return of their sight?

I have attended these celebrations, experiences that I will never forget as Africans expressed personal gratitude to me—but the gratitude is really to all who make this possible. As the drums began to beat, the excitement intensified. People sang with their hands raised in praise—celebrating new sight, new hope, new life.

One of the joyous patients was a Muslim mullah. As I watched him sing songs about Jesus and praise God, my heart was stirred. When I was asked to say a few words, I talked about Jesus and how Jesus loves us all! Jesus did not come for the churched but for those who are seeking. Each seeker has the opportunity to respond to the amazing love of Jesus. What a special moment!

Building Medical Infrastructure

In addition to the ophthalmic training, Mercy Ships offered training in many other areas. In fact, Dr. Hofman met a future colleague while she was on the *Africa Mercy*. Dr. Faya Yaradouno, a resident at Bongolo Hospital in Gabon, was onboard for a three-month surgical rotation with Mercy Ships surgeons. Other West African surgeons were trained in vesicovaginal fistula (VVF) repair.

Obviously, hospitals and clinics are more effective when their medical equipment is in good working order. There were only three qualified (and overworked) biomedical engineers in the entire country of Benin. Capacity building through training of local professionals leaves a lasting impact long after our hospital ship sails. So, Mercy Ships offered a two-month Biomedical Technician Training Program for ten trainees, representing a 300% increase in national capacity!

Poverty and disease play a significant role in affecting mental health. Ironically, where there is a higher rate of poverty, there is a distinct lack of mental health care. Mercy Ships provided a ten-week Mental Health Program to train 100 health care professionals through long-term crew member, Dr. Lyn Westman.

The Mercy Ships Administrative Training Program worked with local hospitals to strengthen the managerial and clerical skills of those in key administrative positions. Participants were hand-selected by their respective hospitals.

The trainees from these various programs will, in turn, train others. The ongoing training cycle will help countless men, women, and children in real need. Thus, the positive impact of Mercy Ships on the lives of West Africans in Benin has the potential to serve multi-generations with the skills acquired.

A very substantial example of building medical infrastructure was the construction of the OSAREH Pediatric Orthopaedic Clinic. This was a joint effort of Mercy Ships and OSAREH, a local non-governmental organization that addresses the needs of handicapped children. The clinic includes a recovery room, operating room, patient wards, and administrative offices. Dr. Seraphin Gbenou, a pediatric surgeon who has practiced medicine in Benin for almost twenty years, will oversee the medical care provided at the new facility. An estimated 215 children will receive treatment there each year.

Food for Life Program

Poverty is a formidable enemy, giving birth to malnutrition . . . disease . . . and death. In fact, UNICEF's 2010 report *The State of the World's Children* indicates that out of 1000 children born in Central and West Africa, 169 will not see their fifth birthday—16.9% of all babies born!

The Food for Life program was born from the realization that health care begins long before a person gets sick. Health care begins with good nutrition. Better agricultural methods produce more nutritious and more plentiful crops, without chemical pesticides or fertilizers. Better nutrition leads to better health. Better health means less disease.

Food for Life focuses on teaching West African farmers how to use the land more efficiently and effectively. The traditional African farming practice is to "slash and burn" the land. Everything is cut down—the land is totally cleared and burned. This destroys the beneficial microorganisms, encourages erosion, and destroys organic matter that is needed for future crops.

Food for Life teaches the farmers more effective methods. Instead of burning the land, they cover the soil with a thick layer of organic mulch. This protective blanket of mulch, as well as principles of crop rotation, produce dramatic crop yields.

Mercy Ships partnered with Bethesda, another West African NGO, to construct the Food for Life Training Center in Hèviè in Benin, West Africa. The facility includes a classroom for training and a dormitory for students.

The program requires a significant time commitment from the students. For four months, they learn how to clear the land, plant, grow, and harvest. Then they return to their communities to teach others. The abundant crops feed the farmers and their families—and provide extra food to sell to benefit the local economy.

A Personal "Thank You" from the President of Benin

President Yayi Boni of Benin has brought much positive change to his country. But in a nation where the average worker earns less than $2 per day, life is difficult. When you have limited financial means, it is hard to feed, educate and provide health care for your family. The ten-month field service conducted by our hospital ship, the *Africa Mercy*, brought hope and healing to a nation where there is only one hospital for every 1,000,000 people.

To express his gratitude, His Excellency President Boni invited the entire crew of the *Africa Mercy* to the Governmental Palace in Cotonou for a formal dinner. He thoughtfully delivered meals to the 80 crew members who remained onboard the ship to care for patients and provide other essential services.

In addition to the wonderful meal and entertainment, medals were awarded. Deyon and I were honored and humbled to receive the Commandeur de l'Ordre National du Benin (Commanders of the Republic) award, which was also given to Dr. Glenn Strauss. The President also congratulated Dr. Gary Parker, who had received the award in 2001. This medal is highly regarded in all nations and is a lifetime award. It bestows diplomatic status and privilege to report directly to the Minister of Foreign Affairs.

Daslin Small Oueounou, Mercy Ships Benin Field Director and former Managing Director of our hospital ship, was named Chevalier de l'Ordre National du Benin. Ken Berry, Managing Director of the *Africa Mercy*, was named Officier de l'Ordre National du Benin.

It was a wonderful closing of a successful field service. We left footprints of mercy in Benin . . . and now our footsteps were headed to the nearest neighboring nation—Togo.

The *Africa Mercy* Arrives in Togo

On February 10, 2010, the *Africa Mercy* sailed into the port of Lomé for the fourth visit of Mercy Ships to the West African country of Togo. It was a festive, exciting scene. Bands played, people danced with joy, and local dignitaries gave welcoming speeches.

The people of Togo had good cause to celebrate. Togo is one of the world's poorest countries, with an estimated 70% of the population living on less than $2 a day. Mercy Ships would provide desperately needed health care to people who had little to no access to medical treatment.

In addition to the problems associated with poverty, there was another discernible underlying tension in Togo. The presidential elections were scheduled for March, and there was a justified fear of political unrest. Historically, Togo's elections were the stage for violent struggles for power. Many nations were monitoring the electoral process. The French even sent 6000 specially trained riot police to Togo.

Uncertainty about what would happen during the election was a great concern to Mercy Ships, as well. The safety of our crew is a paramount objective, so we reviewed our response plan should the situation deteriorate.

Thankfully, those plans did not have to be put into action. The election was held with surprising calm, with Faure Gnassingbé re-elected as the Togolese president. The newly elected President's father, HE President Eyadema Gnassingbé, had opened Africa for our first field service in December 1990.

The 2010 Field Service presented a unique challenge in regard to scheduling. We shortened the field service in Togo to five months so that the *Africa Mercy* could leave at the end of August to sail to the shipyard in Durban, South Africa, for replacements of generators that we had delayed due to cost and time at the delivery of the ship. The old generators presented problems with noise and vibration, so an extended stay at a shipyard was required to replace them.

However, the emphasis on building medical infrastructure did not suffer with the shortened field service in Togo. The Mental Health Program conducted a five-day camp for orphans and abused children. With the *Africa Mercy* as a training platform, African surgeons were trained in VVF surgery, eye surgery, and maxillofacial surgery.

Dr. James McDaniel directed the Mercy Ships Orthopedic Team, which included Dr. Frank Haydon and Dr. Gary Douglas. These volunteer orthopedic surgeons trained African doctors in the use of the Ponseti technique for the correction of clubfoot. For many years, it has been the gold standard of treatment in the developed world, but it was new to West Africa. This method uses a series of casts to gently manipulate the foot into a more normal position. It requires only minor surgery to lengthen the Achilles tendon as the child grows. The entire process requires twenty visits over a period of four years.

The orthopedic team did a variety of other surgical interventions as well. One of the most spectacular transformations involved an eleven-year-old boy named Abel.

The Boy with the Backward Legs

Abel is a happy, eleven-year-old in Togo, West Africa. He's friendly and curious like most boys his age and very active. He has an infectious smile that lights up a room. But most people do not notice his smile. They see only one thing . . . his deformity. To them, he was the "boy with the backward legs." *(see photos 12, 13, and 14)*

The problem started after an injection in his early childhood. Abel's muscles stopped growing, but his bones continued to develop. Without adequate muscular support, his legs began to bend backward at the knees.

In a culture that views deformities as a curse, Abel's startling appearance made him an object of ridicule from other children. They called him names and even beat him.

The anchor in Abel's life was his father's unwavering love and encouragement—that outweighed all of the stares and insults. Abel drew strength from his father. He learned to meet intolerance with tolerance. And he maintained his joyful attitude toward life.

Abel's parents had taken him to three different doctors, but none of them knew what to do for him. Then, one day, Abel's father heard a radio announcement about a Mercy Ship that was coming to offer surgeries—for free!

Abel's father immediately put his job as a taxi driver on hold. The chance for his son to have straight legs was more important. He and his son made the journey of more than two hours to Lomé, where Mercy Ships was conducting medical screenings.

Finally, after a decade of hoping and praying, someone said the beautiful words, "Yes, we can help." Abel would have his surgery. He would have straight legs.

During his time of recovery, Abel and his father stayed at the Mercy Ships Hospitality Center and travelled back to the *Africa Mercy* for follow-up care. Abel was always happy, always smiling, always walking on his newly straightened legs.

After eight weeks, Abel had a third procedure—plastic surgery on his knees. This was followed by several more weeks of physical therapy to retrain his leg muscles to walk normally.

Finally, after three months, it was time to make the long journey back home! As villagers recognized the Mercy Ships logo on the vehicle, word spread that the "boy with the backward legs" had returned. Everyone was curious about what the doctors had done.

The suspense ended abruptly when a very happy Abel climbed out of the vehicle—with two straight legs! There were gasps of surprise, disbelieving stares, and cheers.

And Abel, dressed in a cheerful blue and yellow outfit, was the center of attention. Other boys stood quietly nearby, wondering what this boy—the boy they had treated so badly—would do. And Abel, who had never retaliated during his mistreatment, just smiled graciously and demonstrated that he could kick a soccer ball.

Improving Community Life

Many of our patients are ostracized from society because of their physical conditions. They become isolated and usually suffer economically, as well as emotionally. Many lack the skills and self-esteem required to undertake a business venture. For those who have a job, the time required to travel to the ship and undergo surgery means a devastating loss of income.

Mercy Ships recognizes the need to help patients re-enter the world after surgery. So, we launched a pilot program in Togo—a partnership with Mercy Economic Development International Corporation (MEDIC). The purpose is to provide small business loans ($100–$250) to people who cannot qualify for a loan from a bank.

Started by Mercy Ships alumnus Larry Lalo, MEDIC has offices in Benin and Ghana. Togo is its newest location. So far, in Benin and Ghana, MEDIC has a 100% repayment record.

For our partnership with MEDIC, selected patients attend twelve sessions in micro-business management. Then they receive their loans in two payments.

Two of the Mercy Ships patients who benefited from this new program are Elom and Adjo. Elom now operates a shop called "Assia Bobo," which means "Everything Is Cheap." Adjo, who formerly sold second-hand goods door-to-door, has learned the benefits of having a storefront. In light of her new knowledge, she is reformulating her business plan.

Another way to improve community life—and overall health—was to bring the Food for Life Program to Togo. The ultimate goal of the program is to have a regional West African network of like-minded agriculturalists. So, we tried to determine the most efficient way to bring that program to Togo . . . and eventually to other West African countries.

The answer once again involved partnership, this time with three well-established NGOs in Togo. Nine staff members from these organizations were brought to the training center in Benin to observe and to learn. They will carry their new-found knowledge back to Togo to set up a similar program there—a program that will transform lives by providing an abundant, nutritious, high-quality food supply.

A Reunion with Edoh

One of the benefits of returning to a country is reconnecting with patients from a previous field service. Do you remember the story of Edoh, told in Chapter 8? *(see photos 2 and 3)* Edoh's first encounter with Mercy Ships was in 1995. She was nine years old . . . and she was only a few weeks away from death. A large tumor was literally stealing the breath of life from her. She was slowly suffocating.

Little Edoh was one of 6000 desperate people waiting outside a stadium in Togo. All were desperate for medical help. All were hoping with all their hearts that they would receive a coveted appointment card for surgery.

But in the midst of all that suffering and desperate longing, mercy raised its head. A little girl's gasping struggle to breathe captured the attention of the crowd. Arms of compassion—some weak and some strong—lifted Edoh and passed her to the front of the long line. She was tossed over the gate into the arms of a kind Mercy Ships volunteer. And that day Edoh received an appointment card for surgery . . . an appointment to receive life instead of death.

And now, fifteen years after her first surgery, this "walking miracle" was welcoming Mercy Ships volunteers to her village. Now a young woman, Edoh walked gracefully forward to meet her guests. With a sweet and gentle smile, she presented a beautiful bouquet of flowers to one of the crew members.

During this reunion visit, Edoh happily described the transformation in her life. She recalled how she used to avoid people and could not go to school. But, after Mercy Ships entered her life, everything changed for the better. Now she can go everywhere, including school.

In fact, Edoh is a good student. After she completes her secondary education, she wants to become a nurse to help others—just like she was helped.

The celebration arranged by Edoh's family culminated at the cascade, a beautiful waterfall that roars down the mountain behind their home. There, her brothers played their native drums, and everyone sang praises to God for His mercy toward Edoh.

A smiling Edoh said, "If it wasn't for Mercy Ships, I would be dead. Mercy Ships changed that. I used to look in the mirror and feel pity for myself. But now I think about what happened to me, and it's all about God. I put everything in God's hands."

This joyful reunion with Edoh was one of many bright moments during our time in Togo.

Lunch with the Togolese Minister of Health

As the field service drew to a close, the Senior Management Team onboard the *Africa Mercy* received an invitation to have lunch with the Togolese Minister of Health. When they arrived, they discovered that a ceremony was being held in honor of Mercy Ships service in bringing hope and healing to Togo. The team received medals presented on behalf of the President of Togo.

The *Africa Mercy* had served well in Liberia, Benin, and Togo. Now she was going to South Africa for installation of cost-reducing, emissions-lowering new generators.

SHIP'S LOG:
2010–2012

● ● ●

Durban, South Africa
29° 53' S, 31° 03' E

Freetown, Sierra Leone
08° 30' N, 13° 15' W

Lomé, Togo
06° 10' N, 01° 21' E

CHAPTER 16

CAPACITY BUILDING AND NEW POWER

The only way to be truly satisfied is to do what you believe is great work. And the only way to do great work is to love what you do. If you haven't found it yet, keep looking. Don't settle. As with all matters of the heart, you'll know when you find it.

—Steve Jobs

Following the successful field service in Togo, the *Africa Mercy* sailed to Durban, South Africa, to spend three months in shipyard having new generators installed. During that time, Mercy Ships offered land-based dental services and training, eye surgeries and training, and mental health training—benefiting thousands of people in the provinces of the Eastern Cape and KwaZulu Natal, South Africa.

Accomplishing both the shipyard and program objectives required creativity and flexibility. The first order of business was to relocate the crew. Approximately 100 of the adult crew, plus children, were moved ashore to a facility at Appelsbosch. Everyone quickly settled into their temporary "new" home. The children in the Academy hosted an Open

House to display their class projects. Alex Williams and Sharon Ruggles, a couple who had met one year previously during their service with Mercy Ships, were married in the amphitheater at Appelsbosch.

Shipyard Projects

Of course, the main shipyard project was installing four new, fuel-efficient MAN generators. They reduce our fuel consumption by 20%, resulting in substantial savings in fuel costs. They are also more environmentally friendly, reducing carbon dioxide emissions by 20%. The elimination of the problems caused by noise and vibration from the old generators allows full use of the hospital ship's facilities, thus increasing the number of people we serve.

The extended time in dry-dock provided an opportune time to do some additional repairs that cannot be done when the hospital ship is in service. Approximately 80 Mercy Ships crew lived on the ship while working on these projects—replacing the Main Engine Control System, completing a Main Engine overhaul, painting the dining room, completing some hospital modifications, and installing a new air-conditioning system.

Mercy Ships is honored to have several project engineers who return yearly, or as needed, to work on special projects. These engineers often come during their vacation time. For example, Roger and Chris Nowicki served full-time with Mercy Ships for two years. They were also in New-castle when the *Africa Mercy* was being converted from a rail ferry into a hospital ship. So, they put their home renovation business on hold for a short period each year while they return for shipyard duty.

When Oebele Hoekstra, a welder from the Netherlands, was asked why he keeps coming back, he burst into a hearty laugh. "Well," he said, "they have asked me, and the Lord has directed me. It is joy to do the work of the Lord." Oebele is a multi-talented engineer who is capable in many fields. No challenge is unsolvable for Oebele, and he delights in his work.

It takes all of our volunteers, both medical and non-medical, to enable Mercy Ships to complete its mission of bringing hope and healing to the forgotten poor.

Partnerships to Build Health Care Capacity in South Africa

Mercy Ships worked with local health officials and providers to develop programs designed to complement and support health systems in the area. Once again, flexibility and creativity were important components in setting up these programs.

Instead of setting up in one location for the entire 12-week field service, the Dental Team, at the request of the Department of Health in Pietermaritzburg, went to many hospitals and clinics. They provided free dental treatments—1624 procedures for 1232 patients—in four different clinics. This helped to reduce costs and provided training opportunities for six local medical/dental professionals.

In Africa, people often are not aware that they can save their teeth by having cavities filled. They just wait for a tooth to decay and then have it pulled. The dental team extracted painful, decayed teeth for grateful patients.

With a strong emphasis on training, the Dental Team visited 21 local schools and provided 5,112 students with basic oral health training, and 131 teachers received instruction on teaching oral health. A model of the human mouth and a giant toothbrush were used to demonstrate the proper way to brush teeth. When Lucy, an animal hand puppet with human teeth, was introduced, the children broke into gales of laughter. But Lucy helped illustrate the message that teeth must be cared for correctly at least twice a day.

A spur-of-the-moment suggestion developed into a two-day Extreme Dental Outreach in one of the most notorious areas of Durban, South Africa. Dr. Dag Tvedt, Mercy Ships Chief Dental Officer, met a fellow Norwegian named Ingrid Osthus. Ingrid is a graduate student doing social work with street children. The two were discussing the Mercy Ships off-ship dental program when Ingrid suggested that the team come to her church to do a clinic for the street kids who congregate there. Dr. Tvedt agreed, and the dates for the clinic were chosen.

The church is in a very disadvantaged area of Durban—an area that is home for gangs of young people. Many of them have been on the streets since they were children, doing whatever they must do to survive.

A room was provided for the dental team to set up their chairs and equipment. Loaves of bread were sliced, spread with butter, and placed on trays for the meal that preceded the clinic.

When the clinic began, a few of the patients were anxious to rush in for the free dental care. But some were more nervous about sitting in the dental chair. Dr. Tvedt was assisted by two other dentists—Dr. Kaare Nilsen, volunteer dentist from Norway, and Dr. Natasha Rampershad, who volunteered with the South Africa Department of Health for a year. The three of them extracted many decayed teeth that were causing great pain.

Another area for partnership and capacity building was mental health and counseling. Under the leadership of Dr. Lyn Westman, Mercy Ships Mental Health Program Consultant, we partnered with the Kwa-Zulu Regional Christian Council and the Thukela-AmaJuba-Mzinyathi Christian Council to provide training in mental health issues and counseling skills for 120 church leaders at venue sites in Pietermaritzburg, Pongola, Eshowe, Mbazana, and Newcastle.

An effective partnership with Mercy Ships Southern Africa office and the Fred Hollows Foundation of Australia was developed in the area of eye care. Six Mercy Ships health care professionals went to the Eastern Cape Province. Thousands of people in this area are unnecessarily blind due to a lack of teaching and understanding. Some did not realize that cataract surgery can restore their sight.

Headed by Dr. Glenn Strauss, surgeon and lead consultant, the Mercy Ships Eye Team focused on three area hospitals—the Port Elizabeth Hospital Complex, the Nelson Mandela Academic Hospital, and the Sabona Eye Centre in Queenstown. Each surgical site received training in Manual Small Incision Cataract Surgery (MSICS), as well as systematic strategies for elimination of cataract blindness. Assessment included review of cataract surgery rate, patient flow systems, surgical systems and equipment, and surgeon capacity.

A total of 90 health care professionals benefited from the training, and 601 cataract eye surgeries were performed at the three hospitals. The Nelson Mandela Academic Hospital in Mthatha, South Africa, is a fine facility that stands ready to handle the medical needs of the community. This remarkable hospital will continue to serve the local community. One reason that people hesitate to use the hospital is the prevailing public opinion that a hospital is where one goes to die.

Happy patients can change public opinion. One of the delighted recipients of eye surgery was Mandoyisile. She was totally blind when her neighbor heard about the Mercy Ships Eye Team and encouraged her to have the surgery to remove the cataracts. Now, Mandoyisile's brilliant smile reflects her great joy. She excitedly declared, "I had a dark view before. Now I can see! I am happy!"

Onward to Sierra Leone

In February 2011 the *Africa Mercy*, now a much quieter and more fuel-efficient ship, sailed into Freetown to begin a 10-month field service—its fifth visit to Sierra Leone in 18 years. A special welcome greeted the ship and its dedicated crew.

Looking very sharp in his Boy Scout uniform, nine-year-old Joseph Fofanah stepped up to accept his country's flag. Then he marched crisply to place it in the stand, saluted, and retreated. It was appropriate that this young man participated in the ceremony to welcome the arrival of the *Africa Mercy* in Sierra Leone.

Mercy Ships played a very important role in Joseph's life. He was born with a cleft palate and cleft lip. This serious birth defect negatively impacts the lives of many African children. In fact, it is often a death sentence due to the lack of available health care plus the superstitious view of deformities. Fortunately, his mother, Isatu, realized that her son needed a medical procedure to repair the cleft. However, the cost of the surgery was more than she and her husband could afford. "But the doctor who delivered Joseph told me not to worry," said Isatu. "A Mercy Ship is just on the way."

Joseph had his first surgery in 2002, when he was almost four months old, and he received a second surgery the following year. He has no memory of his problem or of his Mercy Ships experiences, but the success of the procedures is evident in his brilliant smile.

Today, Joseph is a happy, active fourth-grader. His favorite subject is mathematics, which may have something to do with his ambition to be a banker one day. An avid football (soccer) enthusiast, he is the goalie on his school team.

When asked what he thought about being onboard the *Africa Mercy*, he grinned and exclaimed, "I'm excited, and I really want to stay here!"

A Traumatic Beginning

As usual, plans had been carefully made for the mass medical screening to identify potential patients. As with all humanitarian aide organizations working in developing nations, Mercy Ships depends on local civil authorities to assist with security at large public events. We worked very closely with the local authorities in regard to crowd control and security.

On the morning of March 7, the crowd that attended the screening was large and restless with anticipation. That restlessness erupted when a portion of the gate was opened to let individuals inside. In the ensuing rush, the gate collapsed under the pressure. Four people in the crowd were injured, and one man died. In spite of his weakened physical condition, the man's strong will brought him to the screening. The hope he placed in Mercy Ships led him to join the long line at the screening. It was tragically sad when his body collapsed almost in front of our eyes, and he was not physically strong enough to recover.

Mercy Ships crew followed protocol and procedures. No crew member was injured, and they took immediate measures to attend to the injured.

The management team on the *Africa Mercy* performed extensive analysis of the situation and worked with the Office of the Minister of Health to ensure future screening activities would avoid all factors that led to this unfortunate situation. As a result, an additional, successful screening was held on March 26.

Although saddened by the unexpectedly rough beginning, the dedicated Mercy Ships crew focused on their mission of following the 2000-year-old model of Jesus in bringing hope and healing. As a result, the medical programs, both on and off the ship, proceeded as planned.

An Extra-Special Volunteer

In West Africa, one of the most dangerous events in a woman's life is childbirth. Ranked 180 out of 187 countries on the 2011 Human Development Index, Sierra Leone is one of the world's poorest countries. The cost of an emergency cesarean section can easily equal up to one year's wages. According to UNICEF, the average yearly income in Sierra Leone in 2010 was $340. The average incomes in other countries provide a startling contrast: $43,330 in Germany; $85,380 in Norway; $38,540 in the United Kingdom; and $47,140 in the United States.

Catherine Conteh is familiar with these struggles. In a hospital in Freetown, Sierra Leone, she was in need of an emergency cesarean section but without funds. The hospital placed her in a room off to the side and left her there on a gurney alone. In extreme pain, she cried out, even though she never expected anyone's help. Catherine was sure she was going to die.

To her surprise, Dr. Keith Thomson, a Mercy Ships anesthesiologist, was touring the hospital. He heard Catherine crying out in pain and investigated the situation. When he discovered that the cost of the procedure was only $100 US, he did not hesitate to pay the fee.

Catherine was saved—and so was her baby, Regina Conteh. It was the beginning of a lifelong friendship with Dr. Keith. He became a surrogate uncle to Regina, helping her along her journey through life.

Eighteen years after Dr. Keith made that significant decision to help Catherine, Regina came onboard the *Africa Mercy*, ready to serve with the organization that brought Dr. Keith into her life. Regina explains, "It is through the ship I was born because of Uncle Keith, and I want to give back. If the ship had never come to my country, Uncle Keith would have never saved my life!" She served with Mercy Ships in the dining room for a short time before beginning college.

Regina's life is a testimony to the power of compassion. Thanks to the mercy of faithful Mercy Ships supporters and volunteers, she is alive today. And she is creating a circle of mercy as she aspires to become a registered nurse to dedicate her life to helping others. Yes, mercy definitely makes a difference!

Dr. Keith Thomson, Consultant Anesthetist in the UK at Basingstoke and North Hampshire Hospitals Foundation Trust, also serves as Vice Chairman of Mercy Ships UK. Dr. Keith has missed volunteering his expertise in only one of 23 field services since Mercy Ships began our focus on West Africa in 1990. Dr. Keith also serves on the Executive Committee of Mercy Ships International. Since 2007, Dr. Keith and his team have trained 796 anesthesia providers (doctors, nurses, midwives, and technicians) in Africa. Dr. Keith is a prime example of capacity build-ing that leaves a strong educational component in each nation served . . . long after our hospital ship sails.

Having Fun with Health Education

Sierra Leone's population of 5.4 million is primarily threatened by poor sanitation, inadequate medical facilities, and lack of knowledge of basic hygiene. Sadly, one of the leading causes of death is diarrhea that results from swallowing harmful bacteria.

A logical conclusion is that maintaining good hygiene is a key ele-ment in protecting lives. So Mercy Ships designed an off-ship Health Education Program for patients to address a variety of topics—hygiene, nutrition, causes/treatment of diarrhea, basic first aid, malaria prevention, and common diseases such as measles.

Health Education training takes place at the hospitality center, now named the HOPE (Hospital Out-Patient Extension) Center. The sessions are interactive and fun! For example, in order to teach the importance of washing hands, a patient must understand the concept of transfer-ring germs. One presenter dipped his hands in flour and started touch-ing objects and shaking patients' hands. The doughy, white-powdered handprints represented the transfer of germs. The presentation closed with a demonstration of the hand actions required to wash all the germs away, accompanied by a hearty rendition of the song "Tenki Papa God" ("Thank You, Father God").

The positive communication and interaction will help patients remember the valuable concepts. Then they can take their new-found knowledge home and apply it to their families to prevent or minimize illness . . . or maybe even save a life!

Training Trainers in Food for Life

Another important component in preventing disease is adequate nutri-tion. The Food for Life program trained 16 trainees from four Sierra Leonean NGOs for 17 weeks. They, in turn, will train many others in holistic agriculture concepts, organic farming methods, and strategies for training others.

Edward was one of the 16 trainees. After the training, he went back to his home in Makondu, where 80 families wanted to be trained. Wisely, he realized it would be best to concentrate his efforts on ten agriculture leaders from the village and have them, in turn, train the others from their farming group. This way the whole village of 500–600 people would benefit from what he had learned. News travels fast in this farming area, and soon village chiefs from six neighboring villages came to ask if their farming groups could receive the training as well. Now Edward has a plan to continue training trainers in each village and then have them train their own communities. The result will be better crops, better nutrition, and better health for the entire area.

Making a Difference for Rugiatu

Lack of good nutrition may lead to serious diseases like noma. Noma is a disease of poverty, striking those who suffer from poor nutrition and lack of hygiene Noma is a gangrenous disease that attacks children, usually between four and seven years of age. It often attacks after a childhood disease when the immune system is weakened.

Noma has not been seen in the developed world to a significant degree since the concentration camps of WWII. Weakened immune systems provide the conditions for this devastating disease. It eats away skin and tissue, often killing many of its victims within a month. Although it is easily arrested with antibiotics, which may or may not be available in the developing world, only about two percent of victims survive the disease. Rugiatu is one of the survivors . . .

Sitting securely on her father's lap, Rugiatu looked around the admissions tent. The shy and docile three-year-old had never been anywhere like this before. Obviously a bit intimidated, she leaned in closer to her father. The doctors and nurses were measuring, weighing, taking blood samples and assessing patients. A mixture of curiosity and fear showed clearly in her large brown eyes. Such a tiny girl with such fascinating eyes! They were so beguiling it took a second look to notice the destruction of her tiny mouth caused by a noma attack a month before. The infection started as a small, button-sized spot on her mouth. But soon, it began eating away her lips.

Rugiatu's mother died giving birth to a son, who is now three months old. Left with sole custody of his children and without a job, the children's father struggled to decide what to do about his ill daughter. He took Rugiatu to a government hospital, but all they could offer was vitamins. They referred Rugiatu to the *Africa Mercy.*

Rugiatu was admitted to the hospital onboard the *Africa Mercy* and placed on the Infant Feeding Program for three days. This increased her weight and strength for the surgery that closed the gap under her nose. She recovered in the ward and returned home with her happy and excited father. "I don't know how to thank Mercy Ships for the good work they have done," he said. "From the first day I came to now, I see a great difference."

Building Medical Capacity through Training

The *Africa Mercy* is a purpose-designed, capacity-building training platform that also provides world-class surgical care as a hospital ship. This model focuses on the immediate need for medical care and allows for improved health care delivery systems long after the ship has sailed for the next port. For some, this ship may be the only model of a caring, professionally run training hospital that they will ever see.

During the Sierra Leone Field Service, training was provided for 13 eye care professionals and 9 dental assistants, and Ponseti training was given to 40 West African medical professionals. In addition, hundreds of participants benefited from conferences that addressed mental health issues, anesthesiology, and midwifery.

Joseph Dumbuya first joined Mercy Ships as a day-worker and translator for the dental team in 2002. Through his experience and training onboard the *Anastasis*, Joseph decided to pursue a career in dentistry and was accepted into a dental program in Hungary in 2007.

Mercy Ships worked with Joseph's school to design a practicum experience as part of his degree program, allowing Joseph to return to his home country of Sierra Leone to assist the Mercy Ships dental team. This opportunity helped reaffirm Joseph's commitment to return to Sierra Leone and establish his own dental clinic, thus strengthening his country's ability to provide for its people. According to the World Health Organization (2010 figures), Sierra Leone has only 1 dentist per 20,000 population. Comparatively, Germany has 16, Norway has 18, and the U.S. has 32.

Joseph and other Sierra Leonean professionals will play a huge role in improving the health care of Sierra Leone. The country's president, His Excellency, President Ernest Bai Koroma, has made the improvement of health care a priority, largely through funding provided by the Tony Blair Initiative. In order to decrease the mortality rate of mothers and children, President Koroma launched an initiative to provide free health care for pregnant women, lactating mothers, and children under five years of age. The government commits 7.5% of its annual budget to health care, with the aim of increasing it to 15%. Sustainability of funding for this program is expected from the extensive bauxite mining and iron ore deposits.

Sierra Leone will be recovering from the destructive decade-long civil war for years to come, but the good news is that this recovery is taking root. It was an honor to partner at all levels with the people of Sierra Leone.

A Return to Togo

After a very brief stop in Ghana, the *Africa Mercy* sailed to Togo for a five-month field service. During this fifth visit to Togo, the focus was on follow-up with patients who received surgeries in 2010, new surgeries and medical treatment, and capacity building.

Abel Returns

One of the patients we looked forward to seeing again was Abel (story in chapter 15). He and his father, Koudjo, enjoyed reconnecting with friends they had made in 2010.

Koudjo had good news to report about his son's progress. He disclosed that on the journey to the ship, Abel had declared, "I will tell them that my life is sweet!"

Abel's face lit up with a wide smile as he watched a very special friend appear at his side. Nurse Anna Parthun had tended to Abel during his hospital stay in 2010. When Abel suffered from an infection in one of his legs, Anna showered Abel with even more care. "My mission was to get at least one smile out of Abel every day. The funny faces I drew on inflated surgical gloves always worked best!" she said with a smile.

Now, looking at such a grown-up boy, Anna took notice of the wonderful change in Abel. "He has a new confidence, and his personality is so bright. Just like other boys his age, he is outgoing and energetic. I am so grateful to see how readily he likes to smile. No more need for surgical balloons," she observed with satisfaction.

Abel told Anna about his activities since returning home after his surgery. "I am going to school, and I walk there all by myself. I am so happy for that. I go to my grandfather's farm and to the market. I can do all of these things on my own," he reported joyfully. Abel also confirmed that he is still active in his favorite hobby, playing soccer with his friends in the village.

Abel's x-rays were e-mailed to Dr. Frank Haydon, orthopedic surgeon from Colorado, who had performed the surgery in 2010. Dr. Frank reported joyfully, "Abel's x-rays look good. We have a very positive outcome here!"

Koudjo spoke of how he has decided to show his gratitude for all that Mercy Ships has done for his son. "I bring people to Mercy Ships who need help. I brought one person with a tumor, and I will bring my sister's baby who has a cleft lip. I do this in my own car and with no charge to them," he explained.

Koudjo has turned his gratitude into acts of compassion. With his help, others will experience the medical care offered by Mercy Ships, and their lives—like Abel's—will become sweet again.

Radiatou Finds a New Family

In addition to seeing former patients, new patients found their way into our hearts—patients like Radiatou.

When Radiatou was 10 years old, a painful spot developed on her gum. It became a large tumor that distorted her face and isolated her from society. Sadly, in 2010, her beloved father passed away, leaving her completely alone and terrified. She moved to an unfamiliar village to live with relatives she had never met before.

Radiatou, now a teenager, came to the *Africa Mercy* for a free surgery to remove the tumor—but she received much more. The love and tenderness she experienced from the crew restored her aching soul and eased her loneliness. They became her new family. As soon as her new friends entered the ward to visit her, she would clap her hands and perform a little dance on her bed.

Within two weeks after surgery, Radiatou returned to her village. Many of the people there had never seen her without the tumor. And the celebration began! Loud sounds of joy filled the air as villagers hugged Radiatou. Many fell to their knees, raising their hands to the sky to praise God for the miracle in her life.

In a matter of weeks, Radiatou's life was completely transformed by the power of love in action . . . the power of mercy. She joyfully told her Mercy Ships friends, *"You will always be family to me!"*

Partnership with Dr. Wodome

The emphasis on capacity building was ever-present and intentional during the 2012 Togo Field Service. Day-workers received training in dental assisting and palliative care. Conferences were held to address areas of mental health, anesthesiology, midwifery, and leadership principles for church and community leaders.

The *Africa Mercy* again provided a solid platform for surgical training for three Togolese eye surgeons, three Togolese maxillofacial surgeons, and a Togolese general surgeon. *(see photo 15)*

In 2002, Dr. Abram Wodome worked as a general physician in Lomé, Togo. A friend introduced him to the special field of ophthalmology and the need for more eye specialists. "It is said that Togo has around 30,000 people suffering blindness from cataracts. This number is too high! We need to help people care for their eyes!" Dr. Wodome exclaimed.

In 2010 he met Dr. Glenn Strauss and was admitted into the Alcon-Mercy Ships Fellowship Program onboard the *Africa Mercy*. He learned a new technique of cataract removal—Manual Small Incision Surgery—that cuts surgical time in half and reduces the cost of the surgery. "With this new procedure, I can remove a cataract in less than ten minutes. That means we can increase the number of surgeries in a day," Dr. Wodome explained.

In 2011, he joined Dr. Glenn during our Sierra Leone Field Service to train another surgeon. He is passionate about passing his knowledge on to other local doctors.

He returned to the ship in 2012 to help again with training. One of the trainees is Dr. Nonon Saa Paulin. He was amazed at the efficiency of the new technique. He said, "The best part of the training program is when a patient is led to the ship completely blind . . . and then, in a few hours after surgery, they are amazed to see again."

This concept of doctors training other doctors will leave a legacy of mercy in Togo and other developing nations.

An Explosion in Congo-Brazzaville

There are two countries in Central Africa that have the word *Congo* in their names. The Republic of the Congo is also called Congo-Brazzaville, as Brazzaville is its capital city on the Congo River. The Democratic Republic of the Congo is also called Congo-Kinshasa, and Kinshasa is its capital city—located directly across the river from Brazzaville. In fact, this is the only place in the world where two national capital cities are situated on opposite banks of a river within sight of each other.

During the first week of March in 2012, there was a catastrophic explosion in a weapons depot in Congo-Brazzaville. It was so powerful that neighboring buildings fell to the ground, and windows were blown out in Kinshasa, on the other side of the Congo River. Initial reports indicated that more than 200 people were dead, approximately 2300 were wounded, and thousands more were left homeless.

Upon learning of the explosion, I phoned Wolfgang Gross, Chairman of Humedica and Chairman of Mercy Ships Germany, with a request that Humedica consider sending emergency medical teams, as this fits their core competency of emergency response. The Berlin government responded by funding €50,000 for the initial team. This was a good example of organizational collaboration on an international scale.

Just days after the explosion, Mercy Ships governmental liaison Pierre Christ, Managing Director of the *Africa Mercy* Donovan Palmer, and I were in Brazzaville to meet with President Denis Sassou Nguesso, members of the Ministry of Health, and other government officials.

This initial contact and subsequent meetings have opened up future involvement of Mercy Ships in Congo-Brazzaville. In fact, after we complete our next field service in Guinea, the *Africa Mercy* will sail to Congo-Brazzaville for a field service there. President Sassou Nguesso has proposed some other intriguing possibilities for expanding our service in Central Africa.

New ideas bring change, and change can be both exciting and challenging. An old French proverb says, "Il ne faut pas vendre la peau de l'ours avant de l'avoirc tué." The translation would be "Don't sell the rug before shooting the bear."

We will just have to wait and see what the next chapter brings . . .

SHIP'S LOG: 2012

● ● ●

Conakry, Guinea
9°30' N, 13°43' W

AS WIDE
AS THE SEA

As I stand on the deck of the *Africa Mercy*, I can't help but thank God for the privilege of it all—the privilege of the past, the privilege of the present, and the privilege of the Mercy Ships yet to come.

A source of great joy is seeing volunteers from more than 35 nations all working, worshipping, laughing, and living together as we share one common purpose—following the 2000-year-old model of Jesus. As a result of that shared vision, we have thousands of African people who now tell the stories of hope and healing that came via the big white hospital ship.

Much of my time is now spent on new ships for the future. In fact, we are currently in negotiations for the building of an additional ship, and we have been approached to study the feasibility of a hospital barge for the Congo River. As I look at the designs for a new vessel of hope, I realize that the possibilities are as wide as the sea.

Habakkuk 1:5 (NIV) says, *"For I am going to do something in your days that you would not believe even if you were told."*

Yes, the voyage continues, and I look forward to exciting days ahead!

APPENDICES

● ● ●

*I. Mercy Ships Vision/
Accountability and
Governance*

*II. What World Leaders Say
About Mercy Ships*

III. Ship Specifications

MERCY SHIPS VISION/ ACCOUNTABILITY AND GOVERNANCE

Mercy Ships, a global charity, has operated a growing fleet of ships in developing nations since 1978. Following the model of Jesus, Mercy Ships brings hope and healing to the poor, mobilizing people and resources worldwide.

Vision

Mercy Ships uses hospital ships to transform individuals and serve nations one at a time.

Values

The staff and crew of Mercy Ships International strive to live by several core values: (1) Love God; (2) Love and serve others; (3) Be people of integrity; (4) Be people of excellence in all that is said and done.

Accountability and Governance

Mercy Ships' core competencies are operating hospital ships and land-based sustainable development. Medicine and ships each require risk management. Independent, outside directors form the majority on the seventeen different legal boards around the world. The executive committee of the Mercy Ships International board has the primary responsibility for governance and accountability. Outside directors bring significant expertise in medicine, shipping, business, finance, accounting, legal, and political arenas.

In 2003, the U.S. Congress enacted new legislation for corporate directors, largely because of the Enron debacle. However, charitable organizations have also had their share of similar issues. The Sarbanes Oxley Act of 2003 has put in place new regulations to assure public trust.

However, prior to the Sarbanes Oxley Act, the chairman of the board of directors of Mercy Ships had already instituted the newly mandated regulations for business, and did so a year in advance. It is our view that transparency and accountability are high value currencies for the nonprofit charitable sector, as well as corporate.

Under the leadership of our chairman, the following committees were established:

1. Nominating and Governance (overseeing diversity and board effectiveness)
2. Finance and Audit (overseeing independence, including an outside auditor)
3. Development (oversight and assistance on development and fund-raising)
4. Organization (promoting independence on organizational matters)
5. Mission/Outreach (overseeing service delivery, training, and education)

Each Mercy Ships national office has its own governing board. The chairman of each national support board may be invited to serve with the outside directors of the International Board when certain national benchmarks are met. Each national support office signs an association agreement that aligns the policies and practices. In addition to the legal boards, there is an International Management Team, consisting of the senior leadership positions within the organization, for day-to-day management and operations. This management team carries out the direction set by the board and also gives recommendations and input to the board.

A charity as vast, multicultured, and multilayered as Mercy Ships International could only function in its existing global state through the direction of the remarkable people who are part of our International Board. What they all have in common are hearts full of charity, souls rich in service, and much wisdom and experience in the realm of international medicine and business. These attributes, combined with their desire to follow the model of Jesus, brings solid governance to Mercy Ships.

Mercy Ships is a member of the Evangelical Council for Financial Accountability (ECFA) and has been designated as a Better Business Bureau (BBB) Accredited Charity. Complete financial statements and audit report are available upon request.

To view the latest list of board members of Mercy Ships, visit us online at www.mercyships.org in the "About Us" section.

WHAT WORLD LEADERS SAY ABOUT MERCY SHIPS

I applaud Mercy Ships in their efforts of transformational development as they make a lasting difference in a world of need. Mercy Ships has committed themselves to the vision of an African renaissance in their vision of bringing hope and healing to the continent of Africa.

—Nelson Mandela, Former President, South Africa

It's not so much the size of the assistance, the magnitude of the resources, it is what comes with it—whom it touches, whom it reaches, whom it changes—that is what true partnership is all about.

—Ellen Johnson Sirleaf, President, Liberia

We cannot thank you enough. Not only have you treated my people and taken care of them, but you have also taught them valuable lessons, the most important being love and respect and caring for each other irrespective of race and religion . . . We Gambians are very grateful to you.

—A. J. Yahya Jammeh, President, The Gambia

Their work goes beyond healing and comforting the sick . . . it provides a sense of hope that is badly needed in the places they work. I am delighted to give my support to Mercy Ships.

—Tony Blair, Prime Minister, U.K.

On behalf of the Honduran people, we would like to thank the staff and volunteers of Mercy Ships for the many touching moments of bringing care to our developing nation. The missions of Mercy Ships have been an example of hope, love, and commitment. We have witnessed the purest form of compassion, giving without the slightest thought of compensation.

—Mary Flake de Flores, First Lady, the Republic of Honduras

It gives me great pleasure to express my support for this visionary enterprise of hospital ships bringing hope and healing to some of the world's most needy.

—Jimmy Carter, Former President, USA

I wish . . . to convey our deep gratitude for the love that you have for the population of Benin. To all of the ladies and gentlemen of the ship, I express my sincere congratulations for such an unflinching commitment on the side of the most vulnerable and poorest of third-world countries.

—Mathieu Kérékou, President, Benin

Mercy Ships exemplifies for me a spirit of compassion for those in need. I personally am proud that in a world in which selfishness and greed are so often presented as prime motivators, Mercy Ships stands as a living antidote to self-interest.

—John Major, Former Prime Minister, U.K.

I feel very privileged that God gave me the opportunity to see that His work through men and women is ongoing daily. Today I have seen a ship and the men and women that take life, hope, and dignity to the world. Thanks be to God.

—Alfonso Portillo, President, Guatemala

For many years now, Mercy Ships has provided medical services for the poor throughout the world. You're reaching out to people in need—feeding the hungry, caring for the lonely, and giving urgent medical help to those who need it. I have every hope you will continue to reach more and more patients in the years beyond. I know you will continue your mission of bringing hope and healing to those who need it most. May God continue to bless you in your important work.

—George W. Bush, Former President, USA

Appendix III

Ship Specifications

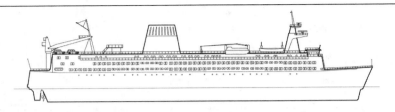

MV AFRICA MERCY
BUILT: HELSINGOR VAERFT, DENMARK, 1980
REGISTERED: MALTA
LENGTH: 152 METERS
BREADTH: 23.7 METERS
DAFT: 6 METERS
GROSS TONNAGE: 16,572
MAIN ENGINES: (4) B&W ALPHA DIESEL, 3120 KW EACH
AUXILIARY ENGINES: (2) B&W ALPHA DIESEL, 2600 KW EACH, (4) FRICHS, 750 KW EACH
CRUISING SPEED: 14 KNOTS
FUEL CAPACITY: 1200 CU.M. APPROX.
FRESH WATER CAPACITY: 950 CU.M. APPROX.
CREW: 484
OPERATING THEATERS: 6

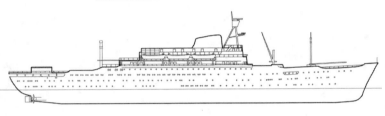

MV ANASTASIS
BUILT: TRIESTE, ITALY 1953
REGISTERED: MALTA
LENGTH: 159 METERS
BREADTH: 20.7 METERS
DAFT: 7.2 METERS
GROSS TONNAGE: 11,701
MAIN ENGINES: (2) FIAT 7510, 10 CYL., 8050 BHP EACH
AUXILIARY ENGINES: (2) WARTSILA 4R22/26, 540 KW EACH, (2) DAIHATSU DL20, 600 KW EACH
CRUISING SPEED: 14 KNOTS
FUEL CAPACITY: 1490 CU.M.
FRESH WATER CAPACITY: 1050 CU.M.
CREW: 410
OPERATING THEATERS: 4

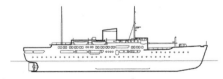

MV CARIBBEAN MERCY
BUILT: AALBORK, DENMARK, 1952
REGISTERED: PANAMA
LENGTH: 79.8 METERS
BREADTH: 12.2 METERS
DAFT: 4.5 METERS
GROSS TONNAGE: 2,152
MAIN ENGINES: (1) MAK DIESEL, 3670 BHP
AUXILIARY ENGINES: (2) CATERPILLAR, 320 KW EACH
CRUISING SPEED: 14 KNOTS
FUEL CAPACITY: 154 CU.M.
FRESH WATER CAPACITY: 120 CU.M.
CREW: 150
OPERATING THEATERS: 2

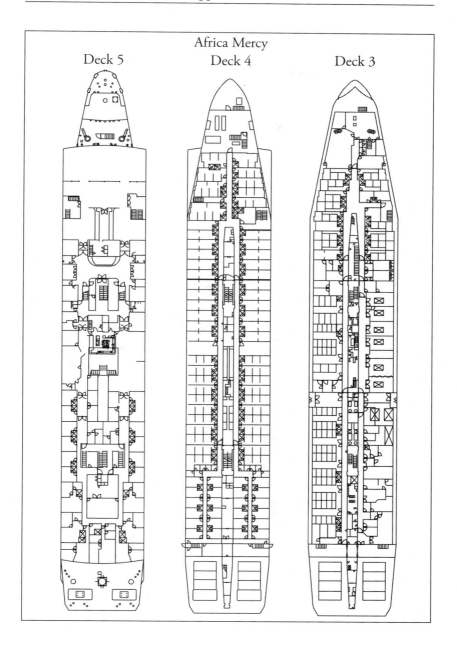

Africa Mercy

Deck 5   Deck 4   Deck 3

Africa Mercy

Deck 8   Deck 7   Deck 6

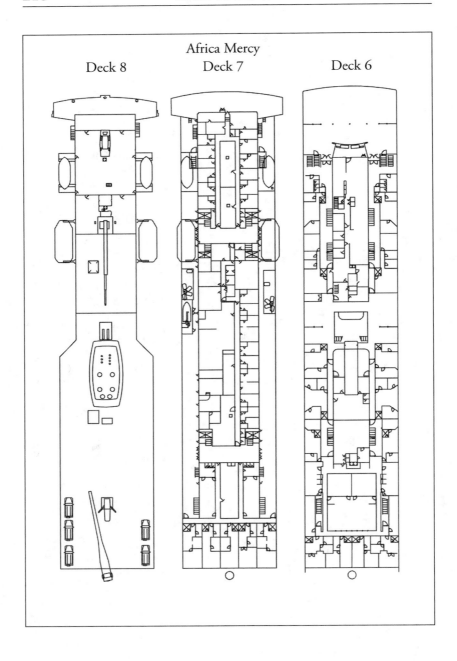

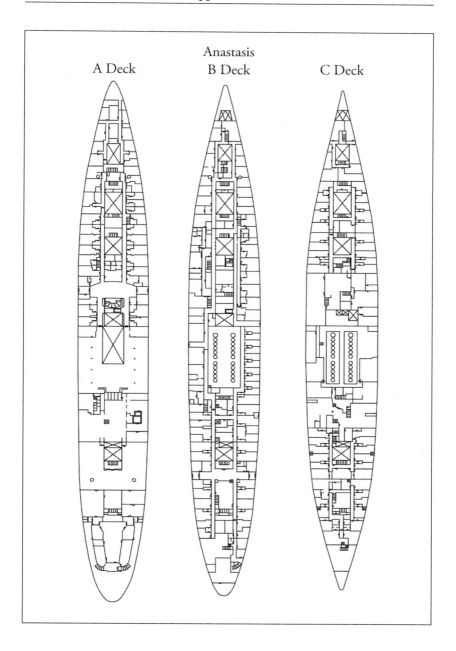

Anastasis

A Deck   B Deck   C Deck

Anastasis

Bridge Deck　　　Lido Deck　　　Promenade Deck　Upper Deck

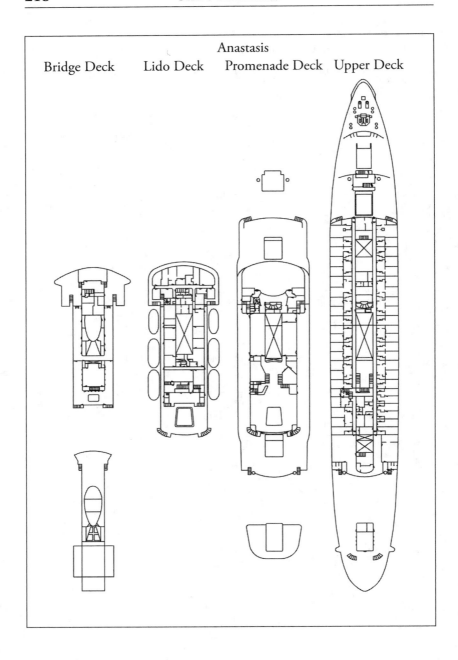

Caribbean Mercy

A Deck   B Deck   C Deck

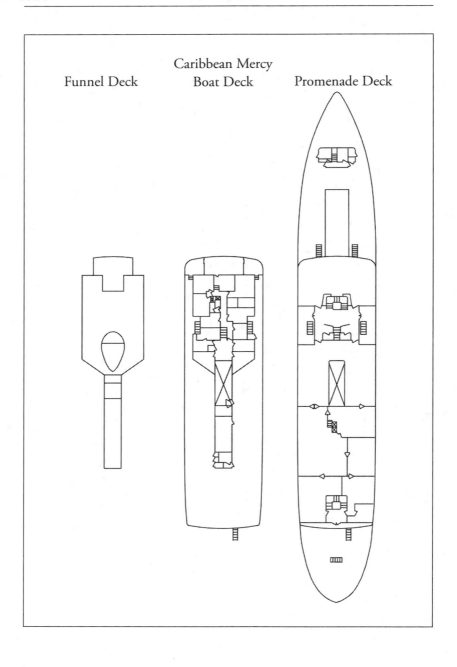

Funnel Deck   Caribbean Mercy
Boat Deck   Promenade Deck

Concept Design for Future Ship

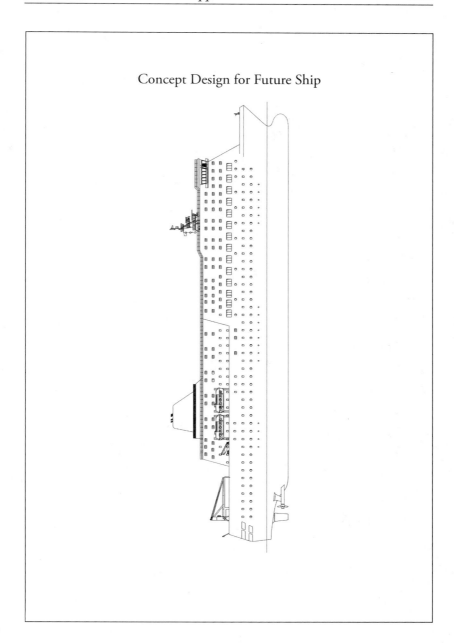

Join us in transforming lives!

U.S. Contact Information
www.mercyships.org
800-772-SHIP (7447) or 903-939-7000
info@mercyships.org

International Contact Information
Mercy Ships Global Association
www.mercyshipsglobal.org
+41(21) 654 32 10
info@mercyshipsglobal.org

About the Authors

Don Stephens is the President and Founder of Mercy Ships. Winner of numerous awards, Don lectures internationally and is the voice behind the *Mercy Minute,* a daily radio broadcast aired around the globe.

Lynda R. Stephenson is a writer and freelance journalist with national and international experience who has collaborated and authored more than a dozen books.

Nancy Predaina serves as Senior Writer/Editor at the Mercy Ships International Operations Center and as coordinator for the *Mercy Minute* daily radio broadcast.